MARXIST-LENINIST PERSPECTIVES ON BLACK LIBERATION AND SOCIALISM

Other Works by Frank Chapman:

The Damned Don't Cry:
Pages from the Life of a Black Prisoner and Organizer

MARXIST-LENINIST PERSPECTIVES ON BLACK LIBERATION AND SOCIALISM

FRANK CHAPMAN

F R S☆O
Freedom Road Socialist Organization

To request permissions, contact the publisher at info@frso.org.

ISBN: 978-0-578-85545-5

First paperback edition February 2021

Layout by Andy Koch

Individuals Pictured on Cover:
Top row from left: Ida B. Wells, W.E.B Du Bois, Martin Delany.
Middle row from left: Claudia Jones, Harry Haywood, Claudia Jones
marching with the Young Communist League.
Bottom row from left: Karl Marx, Frederick Douglass, Harriet Tubman.
See Figures section for copyright information.

Published by

Freedom Road Socialist Organization
P.O. Box 582564
Minneapolis, MN
55458-2564 U.S.A.

frso.org

Contents

Introduction

The Communist International breaks once and for all with the traditions of the Second International which, in reality, only recognized the white race. The task of the Communist International is to emancipate the workers of the whole world. In its ranks are fraternally united men of all colors—white, yellow and Black—the toilers of the entire world.[1]

This book is about the historic relationship between two great revolutionary struggles: the struggle for Black Liberation and the struggle for socialism in the United States. Before these movements deliberately and consciously joined under the guiding hand of the Communist International there were continuous opportunities for joint struggles against the capitalist bosses, going back to the First International, during the Civil War and the decade that followed. So, what we propose to do in this book is trace the history of these developments going back to chattel slavery and coming up to the post-World War II period, and the emerging Civil Rights movement and its ramifications for setting the agenda for a new stage in the Black Liberation movement. All the while our focus will be on the role that the Communist Party played or didn't play in these developments.

The time is long past due for us, as Marxist-Leninists, to make a serious study and assessment of the historical relationship between the struggles for Black Liberation and socialism. It is one thing to say that communists never opportunistically took advantage of the question of national or racial oppression and quite another to demonstrate this based on the historical record. Just because the question can be raised in simple terms doesn't mean that it can be answered in simple terms.

What we aim to do in this book is focus on the Communist Party and its relationship to the struggle for Black Liberation. In doing so we start from saying Marx's premise—that labor cannot be free in a white skin if it is sold and branded in a Black skin—is part of the revolutionary essence of Marxism. The moment the Communist Party emerges in history, it is a

---

1   *Second Congress of the Communist International: Minutes and Proceedings,* Translated by Bob Archer (New Park Publications, 1977), Vol. 2, 144, https://www.marxists.org/history/international/comintern/2nd-congress/ch10a.htm#v2-p144.

testament to the development of a class-conscious working class that sees the necessity of workers of the world uniting in the fight back against capitalism. Simultaneously, this movement recognizes that racism and national chauvinism are impediments to the development of class consciousness and therefore must be moved from the path of progress.

Marx, and later Lenin and Stalin, did not confuse the national question with the question of race. Fighting against racial prejudice is not a revolutionary struggle, per se. Fighting against national oppression is a revolutionary struggle. In this book we show how these distinctions developed historically by clearly demonstrating the formation, evolution and application of Communist Party policies to the oppression and the struggle for liberation of Black people in the United States of North America.

There have been two outstanding, pioneering works on the formation and evolution of Communist Party USA policies with regard to Black people. One is *American Communism and Black Americans: A Documentary History, 1919-1929*, by Phillip Foner and James S. Allen. The other is *The Cry Was Unity*, by Mark Solomon. These books were written and edited by communist scholars and one communist theoretician, James Allen, and they focus sharply on the theoretical and practical contributions communists made from 1919 through 1934 to the struggle for Black Liberation. For me, these books are a goldmine of facts and profound Marxist analyses.

This book, however, sets forth and reiterates the thesis originally formulated by Lenin and embraced and developed by Stalin. And that is that the revolutionary content of Marxism-Leninism lies precisely in seeing the centrality of the national question in the struggle against imperialism and the struggle for socialism. As Marxist-Leninists we believe that revolutionary theory is always confronted with the task of answering the most urgent questions posed by the oppressed peoples and the working class in their struggle against the dehumanizing conditions of capitalism. In U.S. history there have been two great revolutionary struggles: the communist-led struggles of the workers movement for an end to exploitation and to eliminate all oppression, and the struggle of the oppressed nationalities for equality and liberation.

There have been and are various groups that consider themselves revolutionaries that claim to stand with the struggle for Black Liberation. This book is not about them. It's about Marx and the First International, the Third International and the Communist Party, U.S.A. and the legacy they have left us with on this all-important question. In this book we are lifting this legacy up because we believe there are lessons to be learned and scientific principles to be applied in rejuvenating the Black-Red bond, the fusion between Black liberation and the class struggle.

There are many national liberation struggles inside the borders of this country, most importantly those of the indigenous peoples who have been dispossessed of their land, forced to live on reservations and oppressed while being denied their sovereignty. There are the people of the Southwest, who developed as the oppressed Chicano nation after the U.S. conquest in the war with Mexico. There are also the colonized people of Puerto Rico, as well as other oppressed peoples inside the United States: Asians, Arabs and Latinos. However, while acknowledging and standing in solidarity with these national liberation movements, this book focuses on how the Communist International identified the struggle for Black Liberation as being strategically central to the struggle for working-class consciousness and socialism in the U.S. and Africa, especially in South Africa.

These two movements—the workers' movement and the Black Liberation movement—emerged separately in the 1800s, when Marx and Engels were developing the theory of scientific socialism. It is common knowledge that under their leadership, the socialist movement applied itself to the tasks of the workers' movement here. It is less well known, but it is also the case, that the struggle for freedom for Black people was central to Marx's analysis of the United States. Marx was the first to discover the law of the primitive accumulation of capital in the development of industrial capitalism, showing that the African slave trade was the foundation of mercantile capitalism. Marx gave attention of the first order to the role of slavery in the rise of capitalism as a system. He also understood quite clearly that the overthrow of the slave owners of the American South was an indispensable precondition for the development of class consciousness among white workers.

While this book can and should contribute to the building of a Marxist-Leninist political party that stands unconditionally for the aims of the Black Liberation movement, this book is not about that. Nonetheless it is our hope that this book will contribute both theoretically and practically to developing a sound Marxist-Leninist grounded program on Black liberation in particular and national liberation in general.

We are not studying here the resurgence of the Black Liberation movement; however, we believe and hope that this book will help connect the revolutionary traditions of the past to those of the present. If we succeed here in demonstrating that Marxism-Leninism is a tool that we as revolutionaries must bring to the new movement then we shall be happy.

Marxism-Leninism as a body of theory and practice captures the lessons of the worldwide revolutionary movement, including a century of the struggles of oppressed nations for liberation from imperialism. It puts forward that only a socialist revolution led by a multinational, multi-racial, working-class party (guided by the revolutionary science of Marxism) can end racist and national oppression; and that revolution in the U.S. means overthrowing the system of imperialism, or the monopoly capitalists.

The main point we want to make is that history has demonstrated that when the party liquidates the national question and refuses to see and fight for the centrality of the struggle for Black Liberation, the revolutionary movement as a whole suffers. Therefore, we must build the party in the crucible of struggle, striving for a united multi-racial, multinational working class that stands in unconditional solidarity with those struggling against racism and national oppression.

We believe that the U.S. revolution is distinct from some other revolutions in advanced capitalist countries. Here, the multinational working class can't free itself unless it rejects racism and builds unity with the national liberation struggles; and the oppressed nations can't end national oppression unless they unite with all workers to overthrow capitalism. This strategic alliance at the core of a united front against the monopoly capitalists is the only path of struggle capable of putting an end to this hated system. Winning—that is, victory—will require the merger of these two movements.

A Note on Black Marxism and the Black Radical Tradition

This book is not about Black liberation as a state of mind that can be characterized as "Black Marxism" or the "Black Radical Tradition." Nonetheless, I think that there is an ideological need to settle accounts on this question of identity of the Black Radical Tradition and Marxism.

My initial response to the formulation Black Marxism is that it is unscientific. And then I read this from the introduction of Cedric Robinson's book *Black Marxism: The Making of the Black Radical Tradition*:

> This study attempts to map the historical and intellectual contours of the encounter of Marxism and Black radicalism, two programs for revolutionary change. I have undertaken this effort in the belief that in its way each represents a significant and immanent mode of social resolution, but that each is a particular and critically different realization of a history. The point is that they may be so distinct as to be incommensurate. At

issue is whether this is so. If it is, judgments must be made, choices taken.[2]

If this is the first order of business, then according to Robinson, Marxism and Black radicalism must be examined and cross-examined from two different standpoints, namely: 1) Marxism from the standpoint of "its profound but ambiguous indebtedness to Western civilization"[3] and 2) Black radicalism from the standpoint that the "...very circumstances of its appearance has required that it be misinterpreted and diminished."[4] In other words, Robinson sets out to demonstrate to us by way of scholarly investigation whether or not Marxism and Black Radicalism are commensurate. Somehow, we suspect that through this peculiar construction we will come to understand how the making of the Black Radical tradition is related to Black Marxism.

Well, Robinson doesn't waste time. He offers up his conclusions before the proof in the outline to the construction of his study. In his study, summing up the better part of two centuries of the intellectual left of Europe opposing capitalist class rule, Robinson makes a number of assumptions regarding the works of Marx, Engels and Lenin. However, the assumption I wish to speak on is his first one.

Robinson's first assumption: Marxism was founded on the study of the expropriation and exploitation of labor taken up by Engels and later elaborated by Marx's materialist theory of history; his recognition of the evolving systems of capitalist production and the inevitability of class struggle.

However, Marxism as a doctrine was partially founded on the study of capitalism as a system of expropriation and exploitation, or what Lenin called British political economy. As a doctrine, according to Lenin, Marxism "...emerged as the direct and immediate continuation of the teachings of the greatest representatives of philosophy, political economy and socialism."

How does one even begin to understand Marx's "materialist theory of history" if one doesn't recognize that "historical materialism" came about as a result of Marx and Engels settling accounts with German ideology, French socialism and English political economy?

In fact, Robinson avoids dealing with the sources and component parts of Marxism by simply declaring that Marxism is a Western construction,

---

2   Cedric J. Robinson, *Black Marxism: The Making of the Black Radical Tradition* (University of North Carolina Press, 2005), 1.
3   Robinson, *Black Marxism*, 1.
4   Robinson, *Black Marxism*, 1.

"a conceptualization of human affairs that is emerged from European peoples mediated, in turn, through their social orders and their cultures. Certainly, the philosophical origins are indisputably Western."[5] Not really, for what emerged in Europe during the so-called Renaissance was passed on to them by the Arabs and Islamic culture dominant in North Africa and Spain—that is, mediated through the non-Western cultures of North Africa and the Moors. European peoples did not develop their culture in isolation, but in fact drew much knowledge from the more advanced non-Western cultures of Africa and the East.

So, rather than speaking specifically to the sources of Marxism, as Lenin did, Robinson is saying Marxism is stamped with certain inherent limitations due to it emerging from the historical experiences of European peoples. But Marxism as a science is no more uniquely European, isolated from the high road of human civilization, than mathematics, medicine and chemistry.

Robinson's declaration is an abstraction because every idea or system of ideas is born in a particular culture at a particular time, and therefore, reflects the economic system and social knowledge at that historical moment. Neither Marxism nor any system of social knowledge exists independently of social knowledge as a whole. This is especially true given the way civilizations develop and interact with one another. For example, Islamic culture in North Africa developed science and mathematics ahead of modern European states. Ibn Khaldun, a North African philosopher and scholar, was a pioneer in the development of the social sciences and some of the same ideas that originated with him can be found in the works of Marx.

The principal question here is: Did Marxism provide humankind and especially workers and oppressed peoples with instruments of knowledge to be used in achieving liberation from class, race, gender and national oppression? Our book gives a resounding yes to this question.

Marxism and Black liberation are indeed historically related radical traditions that spring from the common soil of capitalism. But they are not of the same measure. The struggle for Black Liberation is longer. There was Haiti in the Caribbean and Quilombo in Brazil before there were Robert Owen's utopian communes, the Paris Commune or the Great October Revolution. Yet the historical fact of the greatest importance is that Marxism recognized from its inception that the emancipation of the working class is the emancipation of all humanity, and that so long as Black workers and the colonially and nationally oppressed are held in bondage

---

5   Robinson, *Black Marxism*, 2.

that white workers or workers as a class cannot be free. This is part of the revolutionary essence of Marxism.

This revolutionary essence is what was missing with the utopian socialists, for whom the abolition of Black slavery was not a primary issue. And it is this revolutionary essence that was betrayed by the Second International or the social democrats.

The Bolshevik Revolution reclaimed the revolutionary essence of Marxism and ended the era of socialism being wedded to the white national chauvinism of Europeans. The Manifesto of the Communist International, in 1919, declared: "Colonial slaves of Africa and Asia! The hour of proletarian dictatorship in Europe will strike for you as the hour of your own emancipation!"

And so it did for that moment of history when the weakest link in the imperialist chain was broken for the first time; when for the first time in history the struggle for socialism and Black Liberation merged in the international arena and became the spark for igniting the fires of rebellion of the 1960s and laying the foundation for Black liberation and the struggle for socialism in the 21st century. That is what this book is about.

1

Capitalism, Slavery and Revolution

Before even starting this inquiry, it is important to set forth at the outset our method of investigation and presentation of the subject.

In approaching our subject, that is, the question of the history of the relationship between Black liberation and socialism, we make full use of the principles and methods of historical investigation first elaborated and developed by Karl Marx and Fredrich Engels.

When we look at history, we see that it is a multifaceted process involving wars, class struggles and the clash of ideas. Further investigation reveals that history is also a law-governed process. Therefore, the approach we have decided to use to find our way through the tangle of social phenomena we are about to examine is called the materialist approach, or historical materialism.

Historical materialism as a doctrine teaches us that, in the most general or abstract sense, laws of social development are also laws of nature, because in the final analysis human society is an integral part of nature and is therefore constantly interacting with nature. Yet there is a critical difference between the way nature develops and society develops. Nature, non-human nature, develops spontaneously and not according to any design or the dictates of conscious forces. Society is made up of people who have intelligence and a conscious will to act, formulate ideas and change things according to their ideas. In other words, people consciously set forth objectives (goals) and through trial and error achieve them.

Therefore, it is only natural for us to assume that society in general is governed by human reason, by ideas set forth by human beings. In fact, the prelude to the French Revolution was the Age of Reason, where the philosophers of that enlightened era believed that our social being was determined by our ideas. Karl Marx, born and maturing in the era of the French Revolution, demonstrated that this assumption is wrong. His demonstration was based on the truth that before people have ideas, they must have food, clothing and shelter. There must be this basic fulfillment of human needs for society to exist, reproduce itself and develop.

The material life of human beings is based on hunting, gathering, fishing, tilling the soil, making clothes and building shelters. The means for doing this production is tools; said tools are created and used by the expenditure of human labor power. Products of labor are exchanged, such is the material life of the people, which is governed by laws of its own, operating independent of human consciousness. These laws determine the objective social relations people have with one another.

This means that in all human societies labor is the natural, necessary condition of social life. People not only hunt, fish, and farm; they produce the tools, their own means for hunting, etc. One might say that a lion's tools are its claws and teeth, not so with humans, who use tools as a means of acquiring and producing their food apart from and as an extension of their bodies. People do not distinguish themselves from animals by consciousness or language but by the fact that they (people) produce their own means of subsistence apart from their biological makeup.

The general laws of the historical development of human societies were first discovered by Karl Marx through his painstaking study of classical German philosophy, French socialism and British political economy. According to Engels, it was Marx who discovered and formulated the general laws of social development and laid the foundations for Scientific Socialism. Here is Marx's classic summary of his discovery:

> In the social production of their existence, men inevitably enter into definite relations, which are independent of their will, namely relations of production appropriate to a given stage in the development of their material forces of production. The totality of these relations of production constitutes the economic structure of society, the real foundation, on which arises a legal and political superstructure and to which correspond definite forms of social consciousness. The mode of production of material life conditions the general process of social, political and intellectual life. It is not the consciousness of men that determines their existence, but their social existence that determines their consciousness. At a certain stage of development, the material productive forces of society come into conflict with the existing relations of production or—this merely expresses the same thing in legal terms—with the property relations within the framework of which they have operated hitherto. From forms of development of the productive forces these relations turn into their fetters. Then begins an era of social revolution. The changes in the economic foundation lead sooner or later to the transformation of the whole immense superstructure.

> In studying such transformations it is always necessary to distinguish be-
> tween the material transformation of the economic conditions of pro-
> duction, which can be determined with the precision of natural science,
> and the legal, political, religious, artistic or philosophic—in short, ideo-
> logical forms in which men become conscious of this conflict and fight
> it out. Just as one does not judge an individual by what he thinks about
> himself, so one cannot judge such a period of transformation by its con-
> sciousness, but, on the contrary, this consciousness must be explained
> from the contradictions of material life, from the conflict existing be-
> tween the social forces of production and the relations of production." [1]

In studying political economy Marx did not concern himself with the laws
of nature—to investigate those is the business of physics, chemistry, geol-
ogy and biology, not of political economy. Also, neither Marx nor Engels
were preoccupied with investigating what elements of the modes of production are common to all peoples, as such an investigation could, for the
most part, only result in acknowledging such obvious things as man always
needs tools, land, and food in order to be able to produce at all. Marx and
Engels investigated the laws of movement of capitalism as a definite form
of social production peculiar to a definite historical period and to particular
European nations.

Karl Marx was also the first to show how modern capitalism as a system
of political economy was a consequence of the phenomenal growth of merchant capital during that period when direct slavery in European colonies
and African slavery became the basis for worldwide commerce based on
the commoditization of labor and the exportation of commodities. During
this period of commercial warfare between the colonial powers, slavery
played a key role in bringing about the advent of the industrial capitalist;
i.e., slavery provided the financial basis for the industrial revolution. In
that section of Marx's *Capital* dealing with the historical period preceding
the revolutionary emergence of industrial capitalism it is stated:

> The money capital formed by means of usury and commerce was pre-
> vented from turning into industrial capital, in the country by the feudal
> constitution, in the towns by the guild organization. These fetters van-
> ished with the dissolution of feudal society, with the expropriation and
> partial eviction of the country population. The new manufactures were
> established at sea-ports, or at inland points beyond the control of the old

---

1   Karl Marx and Friedrich Engels, *A Contribution to the Critique of Political Economy*,
     translated by S.W. Ryazanskaya (Progress Publishers, 1977), accessed July 2, 2020,
     https://www.marxists.org/archive/marx/works/1859/critique-pol-economy/pref-
     ace.htm.

municipalities and their guilds. Hence in England an embittered struggle of the corporate towns against these new industrial nurseries.

The discovery of gold and silver in America, the extirpation, enslavement and entombment in mines of the aboriginal population, the beginning of the conquest and looting of the East Indies, the turning of Africa into a warren for the commercial hunting of black-skins, signalized the rosy dawn of the era of capitalist production. These idyllic proceedings are the chief moments of primitive accumulation. On their heels treads the commercial war of the European nations, with the globe for a theatre. It begins with the revolt of the Netherlands from Spain, assumes giant dimensions in England's Anti-Jacobin War, and is still going on in the opium wars against China, &c.[2]

Even before he wrote *Capital*, Marx had, as early as 1847, come to an understanding of how capitalism and slavery were fundamentally related. He sets forth these propositions with remarkable clarity in his polemic against Pierre Proudhon in the *Poverty of Philosophy*. Here is how Marx stated it:

Slavery is an economic category like any other…Needless to say we are dealing only with direct slavery, with Negro slavery in Surinam, in Brazil, in the Southern States of North America.

Direct slavery is the pivot of our industrialism today as much as machinery, credit, etc. Without slavery you have no cotton, without cotton you have no modern industry. It is slavery that has given value to the colonies; it is the colonies that created world trade; it is world trade that is the necessary condition for large-scale machine industry. Thus slavery is an economic category of the greatest importance.

Without slavery, North America, the most progressive of countries, would be transformed into a patriarchal country. Wipe North America off the map of the world, and you will have anarchy—the complete decay of modern commerce and civilization. Cause slavery to disappear and you will have wiped America off the map of nations.

Thus slavery, because it is an economic category, has always existed among the institutions of nations. Modern nations have been able only to disguise slavery in their own countries, but they have imposed it without disguise upon the New World.[3]

---

2   Karl Marx, *Capital: Volume I*, translated by Samuel Moore and Edward Aveling, edited by Frederick Engels (Progress Publishers), accessed July 2, 2020, https://www.marxists.org/archive/marx/works/1867-c1/ch31.htm.

3   Karl Max and Friedrich Engels, *The Civil War in the United States*, edited by Andrew Zimmerman (International Publishers, 2016), 3.

English seaport towns like Liverpool (which were like little nurseries of industrial capital) waxed fat off profits accumulated from the African slave trade. During this period, the super-exploitation of Black labor was the main ingredient driving the process of capitalist development. The African slave trade was commercial warfare on a global scale, and African slavery with all its horrors fed the revolutionary process of merchant capital, qualitatively transforming it into industrial capital and thus bringing to a decisive end the era of feudalism. Through economic transformation and political revolution, feudalism as the dominant mode of production is decisively overthrown.

During the period of the primitive accumulation of capital, slavery was crucial to the creation of world trade, as we have pointed out above. But when the qualitative leap to industrial capitalism became a *fait accompli*, slavery became a fetter to the further development of capitalism. The more advanced sections of the industrial capitalist class in England became the advocates of the abolition of slavery, forming temporary but tenuous alliances with Black people fighting for their freedom throughout the British Empire and indeed everywhere where they were enslaved. During the period of mercantile capitalism, when slavery was the source of enormous profits, the call for the abolition of slavery was weak, but slave rebellions were rife. Slave rebellions took place along the long march from the African interior to the Slave Coast, in the belly of slave ships and on the plantations throughout South America, the Caribbean islands, Central and North America. The greatest lie that the living ever told on the dead is that slaves peacefully submitted to slavery. Dr. Gerald Horne, one of the most prolific historians of our time, speaks directly to this point in his book *The Counter-Revolution of 1776*, he wrote:

> Slavery fueled a rising capitalism. However, ironically breaking the bonds of slavery was necessary if capitalism was to realize its full potential, not least since enslaved Africans were fiercely determined to destroy the wealth they were creating, along with the lords of the lash. Contradictorily, slavery was both a boost to nascent capitalism and ultimately a fetter on its productive force. More than this, chattel slavery grounded in racist chauvinism—of a uniquely republican and toxic type—was one of the more profound human rights violations of the previous millennium. To the extent that 1776 gave such slavery a renewed lease on life, was truly a lineal ancestor of 1861 and thus, a counter-revolution of slavery. [4]

---

4   Gerald Home, *The Counter-Revolution of 1776: Slave Resistance and the Origins of the United States of America*, (New York University Press, 2014), 125.

Once industrial capital ushered in the factory system, which needs a land-less peasant population to transform into the proletariat, then the material conditions for the abolition of slavery were full blown. It was a cycle or dialectical spiral that developed in this fashion: slavery pure and simple became the basis for a disguised wage-slavery of the expropriated peasant populations of Europe and wage-slavery (so-called "free labor") became the economic (material) basis for the abolition of the slave trade and chat-tel slavery.

In this embryonic period of the Black Liberation movement there emerges an alliance between the white-bourgeois-led abolitionist move-ment and Black people in the fight to end slavery. By the end of this period (i.e. the U.S. Civil War and smashing the Slave Holders Rebellion) the Black Liberation movement (though still in its infancy) takes on the addi-tional task of becoming a part of the growing working-class movement and the fight for socialism, while at the same time raising the question of self-determination and developing a national consciousness.

As early as 1808 Black workers in the North organized the New York African Society for Mutual Relief and later went on to organize the Coachmen's Benevolent Society and, in 1820, the Humane Mechanics in Philadelphia. These were clearly Black working-class organizations, yet they practically addressed the concerns of Black people.

While Black people didn't form a Black people's abolitionist society, they did have their own approach and through their churches they con-vened the Colored Convention Movement, the Underground Railroad, the African Methodist Episcopal Zion movement and Frederick Douglass' newspaper known as The North Star. Howard Zinn in his A People's His-tory of the United States writes,

> Blacks had to struggle constantly with the unconscious racism of white abolitionists. They also had to insist on their own independent voice. Douglass wrote for William Lloyd Garrison's newspaper The Liberator, but in 1847 started his own newspaper in Rochester, which led to a break with Garrison. In 1854, a conference of Negroes declared '...it is em-phatically our battle; no one else can fight it for us...Our relations to the Anti-Slavery movement must be and are changed. Instead of depending upon it we must lead it....'[5]

---

5   Howard Zinn, A People's History of the United States: Abridged Teaching Edition (New Press, 2003), 137.

In an editorial of the first edition of *The North Star* Douglass stated une-quivocally why the abolitionist movement had to be Black led:

> We are now about to assume the management of the editorial depart-ment of a newspaper, devoted to the cause of Liberty, Humanity and Progress. The position is one which, with the purest motives, we have long desired to occupy. It has long been our anxious wish to see, in this slave-holding, slave-trading, and Negro-hating land, a printing-press and paper, permanently established, under the complete control and di-rection of the immediate victims of slavery and oppression.

Although during this period there is no evidence that we know of that Black people are consciously taking up the question of socialism, there is no reason to think that the international socialist movement led by com-munists (Marx, Engels, Weydemeyer and others) was without influence. Herbert Aptheker says Frederick Douglass had a bust of Ludwig Feu-erbach in his home. Marx was a fre-quent writer in the *Herald Tribune* and Douglass was a frequent reader.

At any rate nothing expresses Douglass' incisive, dialectical analysis better than his own words, in 1864 he wrote:

Figure 1 — Frederick Douglass

> I end where I began—no war but an abolition war; no peace but an abo-lition peace; liberty for all, chains for none; the black man a soldier in war, a laborer in peace; a voter in the South as well as at the North; America his permanent home, and all Americans his fellow countrymen. Such, fellow citizens, is my idea of the mission of the war.[6]

From the moment that the insurgent slaveholders fired on Fort Sumter, Frederick Douglass stepped forward as one of the foremost revolutionary figures in the nation, because he spoke for and represented his enslaved people, the most determined revolutionary force for the abolition of

---

6   Phillip Foner, *The Life and Writings of Frederick Douglass*, (International Publishers, 1975), Vol. 3, 403.

slavery. Unlike President Lincoln and the Northern political leadership, Douglass did not waver or become stuck in paralyzing compromise but recognized from the outset that the abolition of slavery had to be the key political objective of this Civil War. Whether they were consciously aware of it or not, the Black leaders of the abolitionist movement and the communist leaders of the First International agreed on what the political objective of the Civil War was, and they further agreed as to the revolutionary methods for achieving that political objective.

2

Black Reconstruction and the Unfinished Business of the Bourgeois Revolution of 1776

In the American Republic, the revolution against England created that political shell within which a second revolution matured. A society based upon free farming and free labor emerged in the North, while in the South developed a society based upon chattel slavery. Each produced its distinctive social and political institutions within the framework of a single Constitution and a single Republic. Social development in the North proceeded along capitalist and democratic lines. In the South, the slave oligarchy established itself as a barrier to the free development of capitalism and as the very antithesis of democracy. War between the two antagonistic systems was inevitable.[1]

From the day of its birth, the anomaly of slavery plagued a nation which asserted the equality of all men, and sought to derive powers of government from the consent of the governed. Within the sound of the voices of those who said this lived more than half a million black slaves, forming one-fifth of the population of a new nation.[2]

As we have said before, this much-neglected period of our history must be carefully studied because this is a critical part of our revolutionary heritage and that is precisely why the ruling class and their academic lackeys have devoted so much time to distorting and falsifying this, the most revolutionary decade in U.S. history. We must, following in the footsteps of Dr. W.E.B. Du Bois (see his work *Black Reconstruction*) and James S. Allen (see *Reconstruction: The Battle for Democracy*), correctly and scientifically

---

1   James S. Allen, *Reconstruction: The Battle for Democracy* (International Publishers, 1937), 17.
2   W.E.B. Du Bois, *Black Reconstruction in America 1860–1880* (The Free Press, 1999), 3.

Figure 2 — W.E.B Du Bois

sum up this period in order to understand and put in proper historical perspective the present-day struggles for Black liberation. Eric Foner's *Reconstruction: The Unfinished Revolution* is also a crucial study of this period as well as Manning Marable's *Race, Reform and Rebellion*. Marable's work is especially important because of its honest attempt to apply the lessons of the past to the present.

We must also consider in this period the relationship between the struggle for Black Liberation and the first international working-class movement for socialism. This is almost never considered but it is very fertile ground for understanding how Marxism developed its understanding of the revolutionary process in the 19th century. Marx knew that the Civil War in the United States was a profound revolutionary development affecting the character and direction of the international working-class movement. Before the Paris Commune, there was the Civil War and the abolition of slavery.

From the very beginning the international communist-led working-class movement was inextricably linked to the struggle for Black Liberation. In the words of Marx, labor in a white skin could not be free so long as it was branded and sold in a Black skin. Marx understood the necessity of capitalism abolishing chattel slavery (i.e. slavery pure and simple) but he also understood how this slavery became a pedestal for what he called wage slavery. Hellish conditions of capitalist exploitation during the height of the Industrial Revolution sometimes made wage slavery and chattel slavery look like a distinction without a difference. In fact, some of the early pre-Marxian socialists and trade unionists in the United States argued that white workers were more ruthlessly exploited because they were *not* property and were therefore left to fend for themselves with respect to food and shelter.

Marx and Engels understood the special, super-exploitation character of Black labor and the need for socialists to address this in order to build a united working-class struggle against the capitalist bosses.

W.E.B. Du Bois was the first to document the relationship between the Civil War, Black Reconstruction and the First International. James S. Allen followed Du Bois with a clearly Marxist-Leninist analysis in his book *Reconstruction: The Battle for Democracy*.

Capitalism, the Struggle for Socialism and Black Liberation

It is for good reasons that the *Manifesto of the Communist Party* does not began with stale, abstract definitions of capitalism and socialism. Instead they start off by stating that the history of all hitherto existing societies is the history of class struggle. Marx discovered that all human societies are of necessity rooted in the material conditions of human survival, based on food, shelter, clothing, etc. and that people enter into very definite social relations to attain these ends. The material foundation of all human existence is the process of production-exchange and distribution-consumption.

Through the division of labor necessitated by the development of the forces of production, communal societies (where the means of production were not privately owned) evolved into class societies (where the means of production became privately owned). Herein lies the origin of inequality, the oppression of one class by another and the ill-distribution of wealth. Concomitant with the rise of ancient civilization is slavery pure and simple. Slaves are the human machines of the ancient world whose labor power erected the Aztec and Egyptian pyramids, the Greek Colossus of Rhodes, the Roman aqueducts and the Great Wall of China.

The evolution and development of human society from slavery to feudalism brings about the formation of classes based on who owns and controls the means of production and who doesn't. Marx and Engels summed it up in this manner:

> In the earlier epochs of history, we find almost everywhere a complicated arrangement of society into various orders, a manifold gradation of social rank. In ancient Rome we have patricians, knights, plebeians, slaves; in the Middle Ages, feudal lords, vassals, guild-masters, journeymen, apprentices, serfs; in almost all of these classes, again, subordinate gradations.[3]

---

3   Karl Max and Friedrich Engels, "The Communist Manifesto," in *Karl Marx and Frederick Engels: Selected Works: In Three Volumes* (Progress Publishers, 1969), vol. 1, accessed July 21, 2020, https://www.marxists.org/archive/marx/works/1848/communist-manifesto/ch01.htm.

Capitalism as a system is often described by its defenders as a social system based on individual rights, and an economic order based on the free market which works best when it is unregulated by government. This definition is designed to cover up the fact that capitalism as a system is based on the brutal and ruthless exploitation of workers.

In a few words, capitalism did not end class society and class exploitation but reestablished the oppression of one class by another on a new basis. Modern capitalism, which brought about the epoch of the modern bourgeoisie, has this distinct feature: "...it has simplified class antagonisms. Society as a whole is more and more splitting up into two great hostile camps, into two great classes directly facing each other— Bourgeoisie and Proletariat."[4]

The economic (material) basis of the class antagonisms between the bourgeoisie and proletariat is based on who owns and controls the means or instruments of production. The capitalist owns tools, the plants and factories, the land and mines, ships, trains and other means of transport and all the worker owns is their own hide (labor power) which they (the worker) are free to sell to the capitalist in exchange for wages. In working for the capitalist boss the worker not only works to earn their keep, they are also forced to work to create profit. In other words, the working day is divided into two parts: paid and unpaid labor. The unpaid part of the working day is that part where the worker literally slaves for the capitalist boss.

In the initial stages of industrial capitalism, workers worked for 12 and 14 hours a day and earned just enough to stay alive and get back to work. Their associated productive activities produced vast sums of wealth for the capitalists while the workers sank deeper and deeper into poverty. They (the workers) were exploited in such a manner that their exploitation created surplus value and thus the fruits of their labor would enrich the capitalist bosses. The workers became conscious of the fact that they were being exploited as associated producers and so they joined together in fighting for a shorter working day and higher wages. At this instinctive level of class struggle, workers begin to form unions, learn to withhold their labor and carry on campaigns to influence the political process, including getting laws passed that would improve wages and better working conditions.

The struggle between the capitalist class and the working class is the axis around which all ideological, political and economic struggles revolve. The class struggle shapes and orients the entire institutional arrangement

---

4   Marx and Engels, "The Communist Manifesto".

of bourgeois society and in this struggle the bourgeoisie uses the state as an organ of oppression and repression. Here is how Marx and Engels describe or unveil this process:

> Economic production and the structure of society of every historical epoch necessarily arising therefrom constitute the foundation for the political and intellectual history of that epoch; ... consequently (ever since the dissolution of the primeval communal ownership of land) all history has been a history of class struggles, of struggles between exploited and exploiting, between dominated and dominating classes at various stages of social development; ... this struggle, however, has now reached a stage where the exploited and oppressed class (the proletariat) can no longer emancipate itself from the class which exploits and oppresses it (the bourgeoisie), without at the same time for ever freeing the whole of society from exploitation, oppression and class struggles...[5]

Engels defined modern socialism in this manner:

> Modern Socialism is, in its essence, the direct product of the recognition, on the one hand, of the class antagonisms existing in the society of today between proprietors and non-proprietors, between capitalists and wage-workers; on the other hand, of the anarchy existing in production. But, in its theoretical form, modern Socialism originally appears ostensibly as a more logical extension of the principles laid down by the great French philosophers of the 18th century. Like every new theory, modern Socialism had, at first, to connect itself with the intellectual stock-in-trade ready to its hand, however deeply its roots lay in material economic facts.[6]

The solution of social problems always lies hidden in undeveloped economic conditions. During the early stages of capitalism, with its crude class oppression characterized by unspeakable social misery, the working class first appears as simply a new order of suffering developed out of the "have nothing" masses of expropriated peasants. Incapable of political action in its own class interest, this new proletariat, this new oppressed order, had to be helped from without by advanced social thinkers and social reformers such as Saint Simone and Fourier. These founders of what Engels called

---

5   Marx and Engels, "The Communist Manifesto," accessed July 22, 2020,
    https://www.marxists.org/archive/marx/works/1848/communist-manifesto/preface.htm.

6   Friedrich Engels, "Socialism: Utopian and Scientific," in *Selected Works*, vol. 3, accessed July 22, 2020, https://www.marxists.org/archive/marx/works/1880/soc-utop/ch01.htm.

Utopian Socialism were influenced by the French Enlightenment and at the same time morally outraged over the social abuses of capitalism, the herding of homeless peasants into the factory towns and forcing them to live in squalid, disease-ridden slums, and overworking men, women and children for starvation wages and the complete demoralization of the workers as a class.

The French socialists were born in the French Revolution and they were the first to recognize that revolution was a matter of class war, a class war not just between the bourgeoisie and the landed nobility but also between those who owned the land and the means of production and those who owned nothing. So, these thinkers and social reformers were the first to see that capitalism was the creator of wealth for the few and poverty for the many; they remain unmatched in their vivid descriptions of the social savagery of capitalism and how these very conditions cry out for a new world order. However, they did not see that it was precisely the class of workers that came from the great unwashed masses of landless peasants that would need to expropriate the expropriators and bring about a new world order. And of course, the fatal ideological flaw was on the question of slavery and the colonies; on this the French socialists were weak. They did not understand the pivotal role of slavery in the development of capitalism and its impact on the class struggle and the socialist movements. As we have seen above, that understanding would be developed by Karl Marx and Friedrich Engels, who saw slavery as the burning question of the day, influencing the direction and development of the working-class movement as a whole.

Quite unexpectedly, and without any conscious intent or calling for it, the French Revolution agitated into existence the Haitian Revolution. Under the leadership of Francois-Dominique Toussaint L'Ouverture, the slaves of Haiti also embraced the slogan of "Liberty, Equality and Brotherhood" and through their successful uprising (1791) created the first Black nation in modern history. On April 7, 1803 L'Ouverture was murdered by his French kidnappers; on January 1, 1804 Jean Jacques Dessalines, the Haitian revolutionary succeeding L'Ouverture, declared Haiti independent, and France was the first country to recognize its independence. The Haitian Revolution was an example of the slaves deciding on their own to take part in the bourgeois revolution in France and demonstrating by their deed that when slaves fight for their own emancipation, no French Republic would be born on their backs.

Due to the conscious intervention of revolutionaries like Karl Marx and Frederick Engels, workers begin to awaken to the fact that it is their

collective labor that turns the engine of capitalism, and that is what produces all the wealth that is privately appropriated by the capitalist bosses.
Now the working class embarks upon the tasks of fighting for its own
emancipation. The fight for higher wages—to be a better fed and better
clothed slave—ends, and the fight for the abolition of wage slavery begins.
Now the workers see the revolutionary side of their misery and realize that
it is their political destiny to overthrow the capitalist bosses by means of a
political revolution that seizes ownership/control of the means of production. Thus, the socialist movement is born in the dirt and blood of class
struggle.

One of the great errors of socialists, whether utopian or scientific, is
that they sometimes did not see slavery pure and simple as an integral part
of the system of capitalist exploitation and therefore did not see Black
workers and the indigenous peoples of the colonies as natural allies in the
struggle for socialism. Although Marxism set forth in clear and scientific
terms the importance of slavery as an economic category there were many
socialists who failed to grasp this lesson and draw correct political conclusions. Here is how Marx analyzed the enslavement of Africans:

> Without slavery North America, the most progressive of countries,
> would be transformed into a patriarchal country. Wipe out North Amer-
> ica from the map of the world, and you will have anarchy—the complete
> decay of modern commerce and civilization. Cause slavery to disappear
> and you will have wiped America off the map of nations.
>
> Thus slavery, because it is an economic category, has always existed
> among the institutions of the peoples. Modern nations have been able
> only to disguise slavery in their own countries, but they have imposed it
> without disguise upon the New World.[7]

What was Marx talking about when he said slavery "has always existed
among the institutions of the peoples"? This means that slavery as an economic category is not peculiar to Black people but has existed among many
peoples past and present. Under capitalism, wage slavery is disguised by
the fact that it exists side by side with undisguised chattel slavery or the
colonial enslavement of conquered indigenous people. To further illustrate
the importance of this contradiction, Marx makes the obvious comparison:

---

7   Karl Marx, *The Poverty of Philosophy*, trans. Institute of Marxism Leninism (Progress
     Publishers, 1955), accessed July 22, 2020, https://www.marxists.org/ar-
     chive/marx/works/1847/poverty-philosophy/ch02.htm.

> Whilst the cotton industry introduced child-slavery in England, it gave in the United States a stimulus to the transformation of the earlier, more or less patriarchal slavery, into a system of commercial exploitation. In fact, the veiled slavery of the wage workers in Europe needed, for its pedestal, slavery pure and simple in the new world.[8]

The exploitation of labor for profit is the crux of capitalism, period. The difference between wage earners and chattel slaves is wage earners have the option of selling themselves into slavery for a certain number of hours during the day. A chattel slave is owned like means of production and as such is bought and sold.

Wage earners as a class arise out of the dissolution of feudalism and serfdom and slavery. Slavery belongs to a pre-capitalist mode of production where labor is fixed in its income and location and is in need of a master. This stability is burst asunder by the free laborer who is neither tied to the land or any particular master but is free to sell his labor to the highest bidder.

Capitalism reduces slave and free labor to a common denominator of exploitation:

> ...the slave-holding states in the United States of North America...are associated with a world market based on capitalist production. No matter how large the surplus product they extract from the surplus labor of their slaves in the form of cotton or corn, they can adhere to this simple, undifferentiated labor because foreign trade enables them to convert these simple products into any kind of use-value.[9]

> The fact that we now not only call the plantation owners in America capitalists, but that they are capitalists, is based on their existence as anomalies within a world market based on free labor...[10]

The wage earner and the slave share a common oppressor but, based on their respective relationship to the means of production, they do not belong to the same class. Again, Marx informs us:

---

8   Karl Marx, *Capital: Volume I.*

9   Karl Marx, *Theories of Surplus Value: Volume IV of Capital* (Progress Publishers, 1971), accessed July 23, 2020, https://www.marxists.org/archive/marx/works/1863/theories-surplus-value/ch21.htm.

10 Karl Marx, *Grundrisse*, trans. Martin Nicolaus (Penguin Books in association with New Left Review, 1973), accessed on July 23, 2020, https://www.marxists.org/archive/marx/works/1857/grundrisse/ch09.htm.

...the process of production ends in a commodity... A commodity produced by a capitalist does not differ in itself from that produced by an independent laborer, or by a laboring commune, or by slaves...[11]

Lenin, in his study of *New Data on the Laws Governing the Development of Capitalism in Agriculture* observes:

America provides the most graphic confirmation of the truth emphasized by Marx in *Capital, Volume III*, that capitalism in agriculture does not depend on the form of land ownership or land tenure. Capital finds the most diverse types of medieval and patriarchal landed property—feudal, 'peasant allotments' (i.e., the holdings of bonded peasants); clan, communal, state, and other forms of land ownership. Capital takes hold of all of these, employing a variety of ways and methods....[12]

Frederick Douglass describes how the Black slave and white worker are pitted against one another. Said he:

The slaveholders...by encouraging the enmity of the poor, laboring white man against the blacks, succeeded in making the said white man almost as much a slave as the black man himself...both are plundered by the same plunderers. The slave is robbed by his master of all his earnings above what is for his physical necessities and the white man is robbed by the slave system, of the just results of his labor, because he is flung into competition with a class of workers who work without wages. At present, the slaveholders blind them to the competition, by keeping alive their prejudices against the slaves as men—not against them as slaves. They appeal to their pride often denouncing emancipation, as tending to place the white working man on an equality with Negroes, and by this means they succeed in drawing off the minds of the poor whites from the real fact that by the rich slave master, they are already regarded as but a single remove from equality with the slave.[13]

To show how this was reflected in the consciousness of most white workers, consider the words of John Campbell, a Philadelphia typesetter and author of the book *Negromania* (1851):

11   Karl Marx, *Capital: Volume II*, trans. Ernest Untermann, edited by Friedrich Engels (Charles H. Kerr, 1907), 446.
12   V. I. Lenin, *Collected Works*, (Progress Publishers, 1977), vol. 22, 22.
13   Frederick Douglass, *The Life and Times of Frederick Douglass*, (Collier-MacMilllan, 1962), 284.

> Will the white race ever agree that blacks should stand beside us on election, upon the rostrum, in the ranks of the army, in our places of amusement, in places of public worship, ride in the same coaches, railway cars, or steamships? Never! Never nor is it natural or just that this kind of equality should exist. God never intended it.[14]

Douglass, the former slave and a craftsman worker, is clear about how the slaveholders and capitalist bosses encourage "the enmity of the poor laboring white" workers against Black people and therefore undermine class unity and ultimately turn the white worker against himself. Meanwhile Campbell, a white craftsman worker, blinded by racist pride, wholeheartedly endorses the then existing institutionalized racist practices designed to justify and maintain slavery.

Yet there were fractures in this system of racist discrimination and oppression rooted in slavery that occurred in both the South and the North. In the South, a number of the slave rebellions between 1790 and 1861 were organized and led by Black workers who were artisans or industrial slaves. For example, Gabriel Prosser, who organized the conspiracy in Virginia in 1800 was a blacksmith; Nat Turner, who led the great rebellion in Virginia in 1831 was, besides a preacher, also a carpenter and millwright; Denmark Vessey, organizer of the largest conspiracy in 1821, which involved the urban industrial slaves in Charleston, South Carolina, was a free Black carpenter.

In the North, though rare, there were heroic moments of Black and white workers uniting against their capitalist bosses. The March 31, 1853 issue of *The New York Herald* reported that "Mr. Hickman (colored) said the colored men were pioneers of the movement and would not work for less than eighteen dollars a month." The paper further stated that to the cheers of white workers this Black waiter declared, "I advise you to strike upon the 15th of April for $18 a month, and if the landlords do not give it, then you turn out, and be assured that we will never turn in your place."[15]

Even while they were denied the right to vote, protest or organize, Black workers who were not chattel slaves did organize such societies as the New York African Society for Mutual Relief in 1808, the Coachmen's Benevolent Society and the Humane Mechanics in Philadelphia in the 1820s and the Cook's Marine Benevolent Society in New York in the 1830s. Also, in the decade before the Civil War, the American League of

---

14   John Campbell, quoted in Phillip Foner, *Organized Labor and the Black Worker*, 1619-1973, (International Publishers, 1976), 10.

15   The New York Herald, March 31, 1853, quoted in Foner, *Organized Labor*, 10.

Colored Laborers was founded with Frederick Douglass as the vice president. And in Baltimore, Maryland, a slave city and state, which was a major industrial and commercial center as well, the Association of Black Caulkers was formed in July 1858. This Association of Black Caulkers was formed in response to Irish and German immigrant workers who violently attacked Black workers in an effort to drive them out of the ship caulking trade, which they (Black workers) had completely monopolized up to 1858.

In 1846 the New England Workingmen's Association echoed Frederick Douglass and the position of Marxists when they resolved that "American slavery must be uprooted before the elevation sought by the laboring class can be effected."[16] But as we have already stated, the labor movement as a whole did not share this level of class consciousness.

It was this contradictory development of the trade union movement that led Karl Marx to insist (in the first volume of *Capital*, 1867) that white workers, in their own self-interest and the interest of the working class as a whole, must fight for the abolition of slavery. "In the United States of North America," Marx wrote, "every independent movement of the workers was paralysed so long as slavery disfigured a part of the Republic. Labour cannot emancipate itself in the white skin where in the black it is branded."[17]

By "independent labor movement" Marx was not referring to simply a trade union movement that fought for better wages and working conditions, but a labor movement that inscribed on its banners the emancipation of labor from wage slavery. For Marx and Engels, the "emancipation" of the working class meant fighting for socialism. Of course, white workers were inhibited in their development of class consciousness so long as their own struggles took priority over the emancipation of Blacks from slavery pure and simple.

Consequently, the question becomes: How is this question of the super-exploitation of Black workers addressed in the development of the class struggle and the fight for socialism?

---

16 New England Workingmen's Association, quoted in Foner, *Organized Labor*, 11.
17 Marx, *Capital: Volume I*.

Civil War, Class Struggle and the Fight for Socialism

Class is economically determined by objective social relations between those who own and control the means of production and those who do not. But as we have seen from the class analysis offered above, the workers in the United States were divided into slave and free and that the class struggle was deeply affected by this division. So objectively speaking, how did the Civil War impact the working class, and Black slaves and white workers in particular?

On the eve of the Civil War, in 1860, the sentiments of most white workers were summed up in the following statement:

> We are weary of the question of slavery; it is a matter which does not concern us; and we wish only to attend to our own business, and leave the South to attend to their own affairs without any interference from the North. The Workingmen of the United States have other duties.[18]

The principal working-class organizations that were white were not abolitionists. Their position was "let slavery be." Shortly after Lincoln was elected president, 26 trades with national organizations met in convention and not one of them mentioned slavery or abolition. The only exception was the German-American Marxists, led by Joseph Weydemeyer, who protested "most emphatically against both black and white slavery..."[19] The Communist Club of New York did not hesitate to expel any member who "manifested the slightest sympathy" for the Southern Slaveholders' Rebellion.

William Z. Foster sums up the contributions of Joseph Weydemeyer, founder of the first Communist Club in America:

> In all his activities Weydemeyer contended for the position that the fight against slavery was central in the work of Marxists in that period. He strove to involve the trade unions in the great struggle. He showed that without a solution of the slavery question no basic working-class problem could be solved. He linked the workers' immediate demands with the fundamental issue of Negro emancipation. In this fight the American Workers' League, under Marxist influence, played an important role in winning the workers and organized labor for the abolition struggle.

---

18 Foner, *Organized Labor*, 12.
19 Phillip Foner, *History of the Labor Movement in the United States Volume I: From Colonial Times to the Founding of the American Federation of Labor* (International Publishers, 1947), 282.

Thus, in 1854, after the passage of the infamous Kansas-Nebraska Act, the League held a big mass meeting which declared that the German-American workers of New York "have, do now, and shall continue to protest most emphatically against both white and black slavery and brand as a traitor against the people and their welfare everyone who shall lend it his support."[20]

When the Civil War started in 1861 the white workers supported the Union; however, their support was in no way an expression of unconditional solidarity for the battle against slavery. Economic fears of Black worker competition soon gave rise to racial antagonisms. Even though President Lincoln declared that the war was not about slavery, he and the Republican Party was still nonetheless denounced as "...the party of fanaticism or crime, whichever it may be called, that seeks to turn the slaves of the Southern States loose to overrun the North and enter into competition with the white laboring masses, thus degrading and insulting to our race and meriting our emphatic and unqualified condemnation."[21]

This policy of opposition to the presence of Black workers in the labor market led to race riots and strikes against employers who hired Black workers. After the Emancipation Proclamation was issued on January 1, 1863, the *New York Herald* and other pro-South Northern newspapers issued "flaming editorials" predicting that there would be an influx of freed slaves into the factories and shops, replacing white workers. Nevertheless, and despite all this reactionary fanning of the flames by pro-slavery forces, objective social and economic conditions (e.g. labor shortages caused by the war and the subsequent rise in prices) gave rise to a rapid spread toward unionization between 1861 and 1865. The emergence of citywide trade assemblies in all the important industries led to large scale development of national trade unions.

Twenty-one new national trade unions were formed during the decade of 1860-1870. If we couple this with the fact that more workers were in the Union Army (perhaps 50% of all Northern workers) than any other class; then objectively speaking, the white working class, driven to participate in the war by economic conditions and political coercion (like conscription and draft) made a tremendous contribution to the ending of slavery. As Marx pointed out before the Civil War happened: "It is not the consciousness of men that determines their existence, but their social

---

20   William Z. Foster, *History of the Communist Party of the United States* (International Publishers, 1952), 40.

21   Foner, *Organized Labor*, 13.

existence that determines their consciousness."[22] Some 750,000 white men left Northern industries to enlist in the Union Army. Regardless of prevailing racist attitudes among white workers, the fact is they objectively made an immense contribution to defeating the Slaveholders' Rebellion.

White workers instinctively as a class knew what Marx meant when he said the Slaveholders' Rebellion was a holy crusade of private property against labor, but they did not have the consciousness as a class to fight racism and racist policies in their own unions. Thus, from the very beginning we see that class struggle unionism and the fight for African American equality must go hand in glove.

That is why it is clear that the decisive component in the war against slavery was the slaves themselves.

Leading up to the Civil War, the slaves and their white allies were engaged in a war of their own against slavery. There were slave uprisings and then came Nat Turner's Rebellion, which sent shock waves throughout the nation. There was five-feet-tall Harriet Tubman, who became an experienced guerilla fighter in leading the Underground Railroad. She was intending on being with John Brown but was stopped by sickness. Slave rebellions happened far more often than the masters cared to admit. And slave resistance to their masters took a variety of forms in the master's house and in the fields, as we learn from the narratives of the slaves themselves.

But with the outbreak of war after the shots fired on Fort Sumter, slaves found themselves in a most peculiar situation. Frederick Douglass best described it when he said that the Civil War was begun,

> in the interest of slavery on both sides. The South was fighting to take slavery out of the Union and the North was fighting to keep it in the Union, the South fighting to get it beyond the limits of the United States Constitution and the North fighting for the old guarantees; both despising the Negro, both insulting the Negro.[23]

So, what was the slave? Clearly the economic backbone of the South, and therefore crucial to the outcome of the Civil War. At every turn of events the slave holders were telling their slaves of the cruelty that awaited them if they should dare to run away to Yankee military camps. There were endless tales of how Yankee soldiers took runaway slaves and worked them hard with little food and rest and no pay.

---

22 Marx, *Critique of Political Economy*.
23 Frederick Douglass, quoted in Du Bois, *Black Reconstruction*, 61.

But the test, the moment of truth, came when the Union Army invaded slave territory. From that moment on the slaves ran over to the side of the Union. They cared nothing about the attitude of the generals or rank-and-file soldiers. No argument or calculated insults could stop the masses of fugitive slaves from becoming camp followers of the Yankee soldiers. Du Bois said it was like thrusting a walking stick into an anthill.

Now the South was faced with a labor strike of slaves. The rebellion against the Confederacy had begun on the slave plantations and the slaves were not passing up their chance for insurrection. They were not waiting on a decree or declaration of government to announce their freedom. Every time the Union army moved the fugitive slaves moved with it, for they flatly refused to act like the war was a dress parade. And when the war finally became a real war, slaves were either received or captured and used as much needed workers and servants.

One can call these runaway slaves "fugitives" or "contraband," but the fact remains they were by their own actions refusing to be slaves. This is only as it should be and can be, for those who want freedom will take it as soon as circumstances and opportunity present themselves.

Of course, what we are describing is the beginning of the turning point in the Civil War initiated by the arrival of these hordes of former slaves, who were more often than not followed by landless, homeless white peasant families. Yet of greatest historical importance is the fact that out of this growing mass of striking slave-workers and insurgents came 186,000 Black Union troops who took to the battle fields to confront their former oppressors and suffered 35% more casualties than any other group.

When the war ended, the working class wanted more of the benefits of its labor, at a time when unemployment was rising along with large-scale immigration and post-war depression. These conditions gave rise to workers' demands for an eight-hour day with no decrease in pay "and a more equal participation in the privileges and blessings of those free institutions defended by their manhood on many a bloody field of battle."[24] Fully aware of the oncoming crisis to be faced by the U.S. working class in the wake of the Civil War, Karl Marx, writing on behalf of the General Council of the International Workingmen's Association, in congratulating the workers for the "end of slavery," advised regarding future actions:

> An injustice to a section of your people has produced such direful results, let that cease. Let your citizens of today be declared free and equal, without reserve.

---

24   Ira Stewart, quoted in Du Bois, *Black Reconstruction*, 358.

> If you fail to give them citizens' rights while you demand citizens' duties, there will yet remain a struggle for the future which may again stain your country with your peoples' blood.
>
> The eyes of Europe and of the world are fixed upon your efforts at reconstruction and enemies are ever ready to sound the knell of the downfall of republican institutions when the slightest chance is given.
>
> We warn you then, as brothers in the common cause, to remove every shackle from freedom's limb, and your victory will be complete.[25]

Of course, these warnings were not heeded.

Given the hindsight of history we know that U.S. workers and the then-existing socialist movement did not heed these words of wisdom from Karl Marx and the First International.

What this means is that during the most revolutionary period of our history—when 300,000 slaveholders led a holy crusade against labor and rose up to create a slave republic—that organized labor, due to racism and its focus on narrow economic issues, could not unite with Black workers to consolidate the revolutionary gains of the Civil War. As revolutionaries we do not simply lament the past failures of our predecessors, we learn from them and use these lessons to enrich the revolutionary consciousness of the present generation.

The Last Will and Testament of the Bourgeois Democratic Revolution of 1867-1877

First let us assess the political situation on the eve of the Civil War in order to fully appreciate the revolutionary character of the war. Although the industrial capitalist class of the North was rapidly becoming a powerful force in the political life of the nation, they were not the dominant force. The slaveholders were the dominant force in government. Let us make the comparison.

Look at the economic power and supremacy of the Northern industrial and merchant capitalists. In 1861 the North had 71% of the population, 72% of the railroad mileage, 92% of iron and steel production, 75% of the wealth, 68% of the value of exports, 85% of the factories, 16% of the large farms. The South lagged behind in every economic category save for large-scale farming (plantations worked by slaves).

---

25   Karl Marx, quoted in Foner, *Organized Labor*, 16.

In the North, the soil and climate favored smaller farmsteads rather than large plantations. Industry was rapidly expanding, fueled by more abundant natural resources than in the South, and many large cities were established (New York was the largest city with more than 800,000 inhabitants). By 1860, one quarter of all Northerners lived in urban areas. Between 1800 and 1860, the percentage of laborers working in agricultural pursuits dropped drastically, from 70% to only 40%. Slavery was gone economically and legally, replaced in the cities and factories by immigrant labor from Europe. In fact, an overwhelming majority of immigrants, seven out of every eight, settled in the North. Transportation was more developed and easier in the North, which boasted more than two-thirds of the railroad tracks in the country. The economy was booming and periodically busting.

Right before the Civil War broke out, both houses of Congress were controlled by the slaveholders' party (i.e., the Democratic Party); the president and his cabinet were in full sympathy of the South, and seven out of nine Supreme Court justices were either slaveholders or vigorous sympathizers. All the committees of Congress were controlled by the slaveholders. Politically speaking, the economically backward slaveholding South held the bourgeoning industrial capitalists of the North in bondage. Through the infamous U.S. Supreme Court Dred Scott decision and the Fugitive Slave Act, the slaveholders were clearly embarked upon a program of expanding slavery and turning the United States into a republic dominated by slaveholders.

Nonetheless, the defeat of the Southern slaveholders and the emancipation of the slaves, given the relationship of class forces outlined above, were inevitable. The forcible, violent overthrow of the planter class and the institution of slavery created a new revolutionary situation that raised questions about how the slaveowners would be deposed and their landed estates divided up among the freed slaves and poor white farmers. Thus, the path of radical reconstruction seemed quite clear: for the Northern industrial capitalist class to maintain domination it would have to take all political power from the former slaveholding landed aristocracy and empower the former slaves and poor white farmers to reconstruct the governments of the South along the lines of bourgeois democracy.

Also, added to this revolutionary situation was the fact that some 200,000 former slaves had been recruited into the Union Army. In this intense moment of history, the previous slave uprisings of Denmark Vesey, Nat Turner, Shields Green and John Brown had morphed through the Civil War into a potential slave revolution with thousands of Nat Turners.

In Charleston, South Carolina, the same scene of Vessey's defeat became the scene of his victory when Black soldiers marched through that place with "Liberty" inscribed on their banners, searching every house, burning slave pens and auction blocks, seizing firearms and abandoned property. Yesterday's slaves, now landless peasants armed with guns, menacing to their former masters, occupying the master's big house, tearing down the master's churches and using the lumber to build cabins, marching, singing and dancing in the streets in a moment of revolutionary ecstasy. There could be no doubt for all who cared to look that the most revolutionary ally in the democratic transformation of the South would be the freed slaves.

To sum matters up. The first phase of the revolution went down like this: 300,000 slaveholders were expropriated of having property in people and the buying and selling of human beings was abolished forever. It was estimated that Southern states had $3 billion invested in slaves by 1860. The revolutionary measure of expropriating the planter class in the South was carried out first of all by arming the slaves, because this enabled the Union to violently crush the Slaveholders Rebellion. Not only were the planters being dispossessed, but their huge estates were subject to being divided up among the former slaves as a matter of the spoils of war. And of course, the former slaves often seized land by their own initiative; as they did in South Carolina, Mississippi and a number of other places.

Such was the general economic character of the revolution. The political character consisted of granting the franchise (the right to vote) or universal suffrage to freed Black men, which Du Bois described as the "greatest step toward democracy…ever taken in the modern world." But no one has stated it more sharply and succinctly as the freed slaves themselves. At the January 1866 Freedmen's Convention in Georgia, the former slaves declared that they would not "remain dormant and disinterested, while you are making laws to govern us under such different relations as obtained in our State before we were freed."[26] They further stated that new laws were needed which "should either recognize our rights as a people, or else the State should not exact from us the tribute of a people, for taxation without representation is contrary to the fundamental principles which govern republican countries."[27] This statement captures the impatience and revolutionary fervor as well as a developing national consciousness of Black people during this period. They were keenly aware of the challenges confronting them and they were capable and ready to enter upon the stage of

---

26   Allen, *Reconstruction*, 77.
27   Allen, *Reconstruction*, 77.

revolution with their banners raised high and their demands clearly formulated.

Because union troops particularly Black regiments, and the Union
Leagues, a mainly Black political organization, emerged as key forces
backing reconstruction and remained poised to quash counter-revolution
for almost a decade, Black people as a people had democratic community
control in the Black Belt (Black majority) counties over how the law was
enforced and who enforced it.

One must also remember the Enforcement Act of 1871, otherwise
known as the Klan Act. This act made the KKK, and other groups that
interfered with civil or political rights, illegal. Certain crimes, such as con-
spiracies to prevent people from voting, were now punishable by federal
law. Under the Klan Act federal troops and marshals were used, rather
than state militias, to enforce the law. Klansmen were prosecuted in federal
court, where juries were often predominantly Black. Hundreds of Klan
members were fined or imprisoned, and habeas corpus was suspended in
nine counties in South Carolina. These efforts were so successful that the
Klan was destroyed in South Carolina and decimated throughout the rest
of the former Confederacy, where it had already been in decline for several
years. The Klan was not to exist legally again until its re-creation in 1915.

The executive action taken by President Grant's federal troops, which
significantly included Black troops, quashed the Klan, thus preventing it
from violently denying the former slaves' right to vote. Once they were
able to vote, Black people proceeded to elect their own marshals and/or
sheriffs in those jurisdictions where they constituted the majority. As federal troops, marshals, sheriffs and jurors, Black people policed themselves
and served and protected themselves from the racist, organized terrorism
of the Klan. To be sure there has not been any systematic study of policing
during this period, but there is a book called *In My Father's House There
Are Many Mansions* by Orville Vernon Burton that talks about how former
slaves became sheriffs and marshals before the end of Reconstruction. For
the most part sheriffs and marshals were elected but in some instances were
appointed by federal army officers.

There are some references on this issue in *Black Reconstruction* (1935)
by W.E.B. Du Bois, particularly in the chapter on "The Proletariat in
South Carolina." Du Bois originally called this chapter "The Dictatorship
of the Proletariat in South Carolina." Why? Because he viewed slaves as
super-exploited workers and slaveholders as agrarian capitalists producing
for a capitalist market. To be sure, Black people were slaves, not proletarians. During Reconstruction they worked for the most part as landless

peasants. Consequently, Du Bois was making a detailed study of the empowerment of the Black people in the South, who were overwhelmingly landless peasants. To the extent that there was a dictatorship, it was the half-hearted dictatorship of the industrial capitalists of the North. At best, they ruthlessly used the freed slaves and poor white peasants as political battering rams against the deposed planter class.

In 1877, federal troops were ordered out of the South by President Rutherford B. Hayes. Black regiments and the Union Leagues were disbanded, leaving Black people defenseless. Counter-revolution ensued, and the rest is history.

The Hayes-Tilden Compromise of 1877 was necessitated by the presidential election of 1876. The election was close because of the brutal suppression of the Black Republican vote. Samuel J. Tilden, the Democrat candidate from New York, had 184 electoral votes and Rutherford B. Hayes, the Republican candidate, had 185 electoral votes, but trailed by 264,000 votes in the popular vote. Congress was split, with the Democrats having a decisive majority in the House and the Republicans controlling the Senate. Both sides claimed victory. The Democrats threatened to march on Washington and President Grant surrounded the capitol with troops. The country was on the verge of another civil war. This crisis led to the creation of an electoral commission and a recount that lasted for months. Seeing that the electoral commission favored Hayes, the Southern Democrats pushed for a compromise. The Democrats agreed to concede if Hayes would give them control of South Carolina and Louisiana. The price of victory for the Republican Party was betrayal of Black Reconstruction, and using government troops to repress the growing, militant working-class movements in the North.

What Manning Marable called a "biracial experiment" in democracy did not end abruptly because of the Hayes-Tilden Compromise of 1877. But the battle lines were abruptly drawn because, while the Northern bourgeoisie betrayed Black Reconstruction in the South, they were using the same federal troops taken out of the South to violently suppress and break the Great Railroad Strike of 1877.

One of the great lessons to be learned is that the principal cause of the failure of Reconstruction is that the North decisively defeated the South militarily but capitulated to the South economically and politically. Under a policy approved by President Lincoln, the property confiscated during the war pursuant to the Confiscation Act of July 1862 was returned to the heirs of Confederate owners. "It is the slave who ought to be compensated.

The property of the South is by right the property of the slave..." according to a Black Boston physician named John Rock.[28]

The Northern bourgeoisie did not have the political will to carry out the revolutionary measures demanded by the freed slaves, proposed by the First International and dictated by circumstances. The Confederate rebels were traitors who were given by the government every opportunity to regroup and unleash a reign of terror on Black people. We believe James S. Allen sums matters up correctly:

> While the South was the main battlefield of Reconstruction, the whole nation was the stage for the vital inner conflict which characterized the period. The outcome of Reconstruction in the South was to a large measure determined by the regrouping of class forces in the country as a whole. In releasing the forces of industrial capitalism and in accelerating the settlement of the western farm lands, the Civil War produced profound changes throughout the country. As a result of the large grants to the railroads, pioneers on the western plains were being expropriated, while farmers throughout the nation were robbed of their surpluses by excessive freight rates. Growing large scale industry, with the aid of the high tariff and manipulations of financial promoters, charged high prices for industrial commodities while the farmers and the small urban producers were obtaining less for their products, suffering a sharp decline in real income. The handicraft and domestic industries were crumbling before the new industrial enterprises. Labor suffered from drastic declines in real wages. The growth of the industrial bourgeoisie set into motion whole strata of the population against the new leaders of the nation. New conditions were shifting the center of attack from the slave oligarchy to the industrial bourgeoisie.[29]

In the 19th century the bourgeois democratic revolution on the European continent was completing itself, and by the 1870s workers' rebellions and uprisings were sprouting up everywhere.

Reconstruction and the Paris Commune were both triggered by military defeats of ruling-class regimes. The Commune arose after Prussia's defeat of France and replacement of the existing empire by a bourgeois republic.

In both cases, the victorious capitalist governments made treacherous compromises with their supposed enemies. In Paris, these betrayals fostered mass anger that erupted into revolutionary action.

---

28   Zinn, *A People's History of the United States (abridged)*, 146.
29   Allen, *Reconstruction*, 212-213.

The democratic achievements of both Reconstruction and the Commune rested on force of arms. The presence of Black soldiers encouraged widespread land seizures, and a small section of "radical" Northern capitalists, to preserve their victory, were forced to support the formation of militias of Black soldiers and the Union Leagues under federal protection.

In Paris, the bourgeois government's attempt to confiscate National Guard cannons sparked the rebellion of the proletariat to rise up and seize power. The Commune they established quickly abolished conscription and the standing army, leaving the people as the sole armed force.

Both Black Reconstruction and the Paris Commune reflected vast political mobilizations of the oppressed.

In the South, although it had been a crime for enslaved people even to read, political consciousness developed quickly with emancipation. As noted above, Black people organized conventions to resist the ex-slaveholders' imposition of racist "Black Codes."

During the six-weeks existence of the Paris Commune, virtually every city block hosted daily agitational meetings, demonstrations and rallies.

With Black folk, mass mobilizations were reflected at the polls. With property qualifications abolished, Black people voted in at least some Southern states in proportion to their population. In South Carolina, they won roughly two-thirds of legislative seats, leading Du Bois to characterize Black political power in South Carolina as "the Dictatorship of the Proletariat..." Throughout the South, some 2,000 Black people won state and federal positions. Likewise, an expanded franchise for the Paris Commune elections heightened the impact of the more population-dense, working-class districts.

Black Reconstruction and Paris Commune governments aimed legislation at comparable problems, including education. While illiteracy was the heritage of slavery, in Paris only 30% could read and write. The Paris Commune declared all public-school education secular. In the South, Black Reconstruction created public education.

> The Commune abolished night work for bakers and infraction fines for all workers, and it authorized labor unions to seize abandoned workshops, for cooperatives and resume production. Reconstruction decrees authorized land seizures, including on the Sea Islands, where 40,000 formerly enslaved people administered 400,000 acres of abandoned rice

plantations until the lands were stolen back when Reconstruction ended.[30]

Paraphrasing Marx's analysis of the role of the state in the Paris Commune uprising, we too understand that every revolutionary, democratic upheaval is often followed by an era of right-wing terror in the form of intense political repression. The Civil War of 1861-65 did in fact militarily defeat the South and wipe out chattel slavery with fire and iron. This brought about a transfer of power from the landlord capitalist slave holders of the South to the industrial capitalist class of the North. At the same time, the rapid progress of modern industry was widening and intensifying the war between capital and labor and consequently, state power became more clearly the engine of class domination. The police, the army and the National Guard were now used as instruments of repression against workers, farmers and millions of former slaves. After a brief and glorious moment of great, unprecedented democratic strides for Black people and poor whites in the South, the Northern bourgeoisie and the ex-slaveholders banded together in an act of class solidarity to bring about a reign of open ruling-class terrorism and white supremacy throughout the land. Marx's capsule analysis of the fall of the Paris Commune was like a prophetic consideration of the future fall of Black Reconstruction. Listen:

> So, it was. The civilization and justice of bourgeois order comes out in its lurid light whenever the slaves and drudges of that order rise against their masters. Then this civilization and justice stand forth as undisguised savagery and lawless revenge. Each new crisis in the class struggle between the appropriator and the producer brings out this fact more glaringly. Even the atrocities of the bourgeois in June 1848 vanish before the infamy of 1871. The self-sacrificing heroism with which the population of Paris—men, women, and children—fought for eight days after the entrance of the Versailles, reflects as much the grandeur of their cause, as the infernal deeds of the soldiery reflect the innate spirit of that civilization, indeed, the great problem of which is how to get rid of the heaps of corpses it made after the battle was over![31]

30   Jeff Sorel, "Black Reconstruction and the Paris Commune: Two Momentous Revolutions," *Workers World*, February 15, 2017, https://www.workers.org/2017/02/29723/.

31   Karl Marx, *The Civil War in France*, (English edition of 1871), accessed July 23, 2020, https://www.marxists.org/archive/marx/works/1871/civil-war-france/ch06.htm.

The class battles that lasted in Paris for a few weeks lasted in the South for ten years. Such are the hard and stubborn facts of history that clearly reveal the objective economic conditions and the relationship of class forces that set the stage for the fall or overthrow of Black Reconstruction and a historic setback for the Black Liberation movement. Yet what Marx said about the Communards of the Paris Commune we can say about the freed slaves and poor white farmers of the South. They were "storming the heavens" in one of the greatest historic battles for democracy of all times.

This is the legacy and testament left to us after the unfinished revolution of 1861-1877. The number one challenge facing the Black Liberation movement today is to finish the democratic revolution that started in 1861 by removing white supremacist institutions that stand with a flaming sword in the road to a genuine people's democracy, to multi-racial, multi-national working-class unity, and to a socialist revolution that frees the human race from the scourge of imperialism.

3

Prelude to U.S. Imperialism

The Political Objective and Consequence
of the Counter-revolution is the Rise of Jim Crow

With the conclusion of the Civil War and the Military Reconstruction Act of 1867, former Confederate States had to adopt new state constitutions to be readmitted into the Union. The Fourteenth Amendment legalized former slaves participating in these state constitutional conventions, which created for the first time in U.S. history universal male suffrage. State laws prohibiting Black voting were overturned.

Thereafter, Congress enacted the Enforcement Act of 1870 establishing criminal penalties for interference with the right to vote, and the Force Act of 1871, which provided for federal election oversight. The Force Act was used in 1964 to prosecute law enforcement officers and KKK terrorists in Mississippi.[1]

In short, Congress was fomenting a political revolution in the former slaveholding states by ensuring that millions of recently-freed slaves were registered to vote and protected by the militia in the exercise of their voting rights. In many jurisdictions or districts the newly freed Black citizens were the majority of the voting population. For example, in South Carolina's Constitutional Convention there were 76 Black and 48 white delegates, and in Louisiana there were 44 Black delegates and 25 white. For the first time Black candidates were elected to state, local and federal offices. In 1867 no African American held political office in the South. Four years later 15% of the office holders were Black; that was a higher percentage than in 1990, 25 years after the Voting Rights Act of 1965 was passed.

Revolution is a process that often stumbles forward and sometimes slips backwards; it is almost never a clean sweep. The Fifteenth Amendment to the U.S. Constitution only guaranteed the right to vote; it did not

---

1   United States v. Price, 383 U.S. 787 (1966).

guarantee that the vote would be counted, that districts would be apportioned equally or that voters would be protected from violence and intimidation. Consequently, even at the start of Reconstruction, with revolutionary measures in place, most of the rebel states sent one or zero African American representatives to Congress. The exceptions were Alabama (sending four Black members to Congress), Mississippi (sending two Black U.S. senators, namely, Hiram Revels and Blanche Bruce) and South Carolina (electing six Black members to Congress). Manning Marable sums up the political profile of Black power during Reconstruction, said he:

> The electoral defeat of congressional Democrats in November 1866, and the subsequent impeachment of [President] Johnson, shifted effective power from the president to the "Radical Republicans." The effect of this political transition was felt almost at once: the passage of the Fourteenth Amendment, which allowed Black male adults the electoral franchise; and the federal government's acceptance of black legislative representation, both in the state and the nation. Reconstruction state governments, as a rule, tended to have a smaller percentage of blacks as merited by their respective numbers in each state. Only one southern state, Mississippi, appointed or elected blacks to the U.S. Senate. Only fourteen blacks were elected to the U.S. House of Representatives during Reconstruction. Most of the states' top offices were filled by white southerners. White historians dismayed by the phantom of "Negro rule," have tried to claim that these men were unfit for public office. Even their white contemporaries, influenced by the deep racism of the day, knew otherwise. Four of the sixteen elected to Congress had received college diplomas; five were prominent lawyers. Francis L. Cordozo, who served as South Carolina's secretary of state from 1868-1872, was a former student of the University of Glasgow. Mississippi's two Black U.S. Senators, Hiram R. Revels and Blanche K. Bruce, were superior in intellect and political acumen to most of their counterparts. Revels was trained in an Ohio seminary and attended Knox College in Illinois. During the war he served as a tax collector, sheriff and superintendent of schools before his election to the U.S. Senate in 1874. He purchased hundreds of acres of farmland in the state's "black belt" region and became one of the most affluent public figures in the South. Between 1869 and 1901, a total of 816 black men were elected as federal and state legislators. Of these, 63 percent came from just four southern states: South Carolina (218); Virginia (93); North Carolina (82); and Louisiana (122). Some southern and border

states with substantial black populations had few or no black elected officials: Kentucky (0); Maryland (0); Tennessee (12); West Virginia (1).[2]

Today we have only three African Americans in the U.S. Senate; and only a handful have been elected since Reconstruction.

But even these less-than-sweeping reforms gave rise to fierce political reaction of the former slaveholders who wanted to immediately stage a violent counter-revolution under the leadership of former Confederate officers and the Knights of the White Camellia. These were white supremacist, terrorist groups first organized by former Confederate Generals George Gordon and Nathan Bedford Forrest, and other Confederate veterans and rich planters. By violence and intimidation these racist groups prevented the enforcement of the Fifteenth Amendment.

In 1876 the U.S. Supreme Court[3] narrowed the scope of the Enforcement Act and the Force Act by holding that the due process and equal protection clauses of the Fourteenth Amendment applied only to state action and not the action of individuals, thus paving the way of giving the white, minority former slaveholders political control of the Southern states. For the most part, illegal means were used to establish white political supremacy. First terroristic violence (i.e., murder and intimidation) was used to suppress Black voter turnout, and second, once in office white elected officials and politicians proceeded to enact and enforce disfranchising laws such as poll taxes, literacy tests, vouchers of 'good character,' and disqualification for 'crimes of turpitude.' The political process utilizing all these tactics was called "Redemption."

In order to convey a real sense of the South's political reaction, let us take the words of President Grant himself describing conditions in Louisiana. Grant wrote to the U.S. Senate, January 13, 1875, the following:

> On the 13th of April 1873…a butchery of citizens was committed at Colfax [Louisiana], which in blood-thirstiness and barbarity is hardly surpassed by any acts of savage warfare…Insuperable obstructions were thrown in the way of punishing these murderers, and the so-called conservative papers not only justified the massacre [of over 105 African Americans in an effort to unseat duly elected Black office holders] but announced as Federal tyranny and despotism the attempt of the United States officers to bring them to justice.[4]

---

2   Manning Marable, *Race, Reform and Rebellion: The Second Reconstruction and Beyond in Black America*, 1945-2006, 3rd ed., (University Press of Mississippi 2007), 7-8.
3   United States v. Cruikshank, 92 U.S. 542 (1875).
4   Du Bois, *Black Reconstruction*, 685.

Some of these murderers were charged but the U.S. Supreme Court in the *Cruikshank* decision cited above found the indictments faulty and no one was successfully prosecuted.

It was by these methods of politically motivated terrorism that the Reconstruction governments were overthrown, and Black people were disfranchised. In 1875 President Grant refused to send federal troops into Mississippi. In 1876 the presidential election between Hayes and Tilden was undecided; the Democrats agreed to concede if Hayes would promise to withdraw federal troops from the South. Hence, the fatal blow to Black Reconstruction was delivered.

In 1877 President Rutherford B. Hayes ordered the federal troops out of the South, thus allowing the white, racist minority of ex-slaveholders to continue to seize political power and use the state as an instrument for disfranchising African Americans.

In the eyes of the planter class (who were simply agrarian capitalists exploiting slave labor) the worst thing that came out of the Civil War was freeing the slaves (which meant that Black people could no longer be bought and sold like farm chattel) and, after that, transforming them into free, educated, voting citizens. As far as ex-slaveholders were concerned this meant the eventual ruin of all civilization.

The rich, white planters, though a minority, were able to win over to their ideals the vast majority of poor whites. In other words, the rich whites of the South promised the poor, ignorant and impoverished whites that their problems would be addressed through white unity against African Americans.

This kind of clearly stated and organized racist politics set the stage for the enactment of Black Codes for legalizing racism and pushing Black workers to the bottom and making them super-exploited workers, and for the creation of a class locked in semi-feudal property relations in the planter-dominated countryside.

So not only were Black people denied the vote, they were forced back into the cotton fields under slave-like conditions that turned the South into a medieval torture chamber. W.E.B. Du Bois, in his already cited work, *Black Reconstruction,* points out, "Finally the poor whites joined the sons of the planters and disenfranchised the black laborer, thus nullifying the labor movement in the South for a half century and more."[5] In fact, one might add that this gutting of democracy and the economic, cultural and social retardation it caused in the South continues to this day as one

---

5   Du Bois, *Black Reconstruction*, 131.

of the main roadblocks to all progressive and working-class struggles in the United States.

In 1890 the state of Louisiana passed a law known as the Separate Car Act, which required Black and white people to ride in separate railroad cars. An interracial group of New Orleans residents formed the *Comité des Citoyens* (Committee of Citizens) dedicated to repealing this racist law. The challenge came as a result of Homer Adolph Plessy being arrested for taking a seat in a white-only car. It was argued in court that the Separate Car Act was unconstitutional because it denied citizen Plessy his right pursuant to the Thirteenth and Fourteenth Amendments to the U.S. Constitution. The presiding judge was John Howard Ferguson, who ruled that Louisiana could regulate railroad companies within its borders. This decision was later upheld by the U.S. Supreme Court, which accepted racial segregation under the "separate but equal" doctrine. Thus, legally began the era of Jim Crow, i.e., racial segregation in public facilities.

On November 4, 1898, *The Raleigh News and Observer* newspaper noted, "The First Red Shirt parade [the Red Shirts were avowed white supremacists and a paramilitary group used by Southern Democrats] on horseback ever witnessed in Wilmington, North Carolina electrified the people today. It created enthusiasm among the whites and consternation among the Negroes. The whole town turned out to see it. It was an enthusiastic body of men."[6]

Six days after this parade and rally the Red Shirt plan to overthrow the duly elected local government of Black and white Republicans in Wilmington, North Carolina was successfully carried out. This was the first admitted coup d'état in U.S. history.

Thus, by these dastardly means the Northern capitalist and Southern planter slaughtered democracy in the South and crippled it in the nation. Yet it must be acknowledged that in less than a decade Black people played a revolutionary role in the battle for democracy during Reconstruction. Here were a people fresh out of 250 years of bondage that achieved remarkable democratic gains even though they were betrayed by Republicans and threatened with extermination by Democrats. Black people became aware quite quickly of how to use their political power as an instrument of their liberation. In ten years, they made 100 years of history. In the words of Tourgee, a famous carpetbagger,

> They instituted a public-school system in a realm where public schools had been unknown. They opened the ballot box and jury box to

---

6   "Wilmington Red Shirts," *The Raleigh News and Observer*, November 4, 1898.

thousands of white men who had been debarred from them by a lack of earthly possessions. They introduced home rule in the South. They abolished the whipping post, and branding iron the stock and other barbarous forms of punishment which had up to that time prevailed. They reduced capital felonies from about twenty to two or three. In an age of extravagance, they were not extravagant in the sums appropriated for public works. In all that time no man's rights of person were invaded under the forms of laws.[7]

With what Du Bois called the "counter-revolution of property," the planter class overthrew what might have become the cornerstone of bourgeois democracy, the enfranchisement of former slaves and poor white farmers. This counter-revolution thereby turned the whole spiritual and economic (material) development in a reactionary direction predicated on the disfranchisement of Black people in the South and the brutal suppression of working-class rebellions against the rapidly rising monopoly capitalists of the North.

Du Bois wrote that the United States,

> ... became the cornerstone of that new imperialism which is subjecting the labor of yellow, brown and black peoples to the dictation of capitalism on a world basis; and it has not only brought nearer the revolution by which the power of capitalism is to be challenged, but also it is transforming the fight to the sinister aspect of a fight on racial lines embittered by awful memories.[8]

By 1910 the United States was an undisputed imperialist power and Jim Crow, the racist institution of the South, was a *fait accompli*. Racial segregation was legal and spread like a cancer throughout the land. Jim Crow policies and denying the voting rights of African Americans prevailed despite periodic legal challenges in court.

Not until the Civil Rights Congress started organizing against lynching (from the 1930s through the 1950s), the U.S Supreme Court's decision of *Brown v. Board of Education*, and Rosa Parks' refusal to give up her seat on the bus, do we see any prospect or hope for federal intervention. From the very beginning one of the primary goals of the Civil Rights movement was restoring the voting rights of Black people, which were taken because of the overthrow of the Black Reconstruction governments of the South.

---

7   Du Bois, *Black Reconstruction*, 621.
8   Du Bois, *Black Reconstruction*, 631.

4

Jim Crow and the Moribund Stage of Capitalism

Jim Crow was ushered in by the counter-revolution in the South led by the former slaveholders and ex-Confederate generals. The Tilden-Hayes Compromise of 1877 signaled the birth of Jim Crow with its legalized racial segregation, lynching and pogroms. The South became that quadrant of the United States that was operated along the lines of a police state, pure and simple. During the same period, the United States became an imperial power in the wake of the Spanish-American War. The old colonial powers of Europe were losing their grip in the New World and the collapse of the Spanish empire in the Americas and the South Pacific gave the United States the opportunity it needed to become a new imperial power in the world. For the U.S.A., the Spanish-American war announced the arrival of imperialism and a new stage in capitalist development.

Lenin offers the following definition of imperialism:

> ... very brief definitions, although convenient, for they sum up the main points, are nevertheless inadequate, since we have to deduce from them some especially important features of the phenomenon that has to be defined. And so, without forgetting the conditional and relative value of all definitions in general, which can never embrace all the concatenations of a phenomenon in its full development, we must give a definition of imperialism that will include the following five of its basic features:
>
> (1) The concentration of production and capital has developed to such a high stage that it has created monopolies which play a decisive role in economic life; (2) the merging of bank capital with industrial capital, and the creation, on the basis of this "finance capital," of a financial oligarchy; (3) the export of capital as distinguished from the export of commodities acquires exceptional importance; (4) the formation of international monopolist capitalist associations which share the world among themselves, and (5) the territorial division of the whole world among the biggest capitalist powers is completed. Imperialism is capitalism at that stage of development at which the dominance of monopolies

and finance capital is established; in which the export of capital has acquired pronounced importance; in which the division of the world among the international trusts has begun, in which the division of all territories of the globe among the biggest capitalist powers has been completed.[1]

The economic, material basis for imperialism was greatly stimulated by the Civil War. In the wake of this momentous political revolution U.S. industrial capitalism made great strides. Freed from the albatross of chattel slavery around its neck, industrial capitalism broke loose into galloping strides. Production in mining, railroad and steel skyrocketed. From 1860 to 1900 the national wealth increased from $16 billion to $88 billion. Capital invested went up 450% and the value of manufacturing soared upward 500%. There were profits like the world had never seen before; the population increased by 150% and the number of workers increased by 325%. Trust-building and concentration and monopolization of capital were rapidly becoming dominant features of the economy.

William Z. Foster sums up these developments and this crucial turning point in our history in the following manner:

> In the process of trustifying the great industrial network had largely fallen under the control of a few huge banking-industrial concerns-finance capitalists; namely Morgan, Rockefeller, Melon, Vanderbilt, Kuhn-Loeb and others. These wealthy capitalist overlords had also come to dominate the national government. Their marked advance onto the world scene as militant imperialists aiming at the conquest and robbing of colonial peoples was during the Spanish American war of 1898. In this war (deliberately provoked by imperialist Washington), the militant young United States stripped decrepit old Spain of the Philippines, Cuba and Puerto Rico—the last remnants of its once vast American and Asian colonial empire.[2]

The prerequisite for this increased wealth and power of the capitalist bosses was the increased exploitation and impoverishment of the working class as well as small farmers and toilers of the soil and the shameless brutal oppression of Black people reinforced in the South by a system of racial

---

1   Vladimir Lenin, "Imperialism the Highest Stage of Capitalism", in *Selected Works* (Progress Publishers, 1963), vol. 1, accessed August 30, 2020, https://www.marxists.org/archive/lenin/works/1916/imp-hsc/ch07.htm.

2   William Z. Foster, *The Negro People in American History* (International Publishers, 1976), 388.

segregation and the reign of racist terror. Foster describes the plight of the farmers in this period, said he:

> The pattern that the new monopolists sought to introduce among the workers of the soil was closely akin to the special American type of serfdom that they were trying to fasten upon the industrial workers. Their general aim was to take away the farms and reduce the farmers to a state of tenancy, not much better than that of the Southern sharecroppers. Their means to this end was a monopolistic control of freight rates, credit rates, and the prices of all those commodities that the poorer farmer had to buy or sell. On every side the farmers were confronted by ruthless monopolies which strove to suck them dry.[3]

The white workers also lived a miserable existence under the iron heel of the monopoly capitalists and Wall Street bankers, some in company-owned towns throughout the hinterlands of America.

The monopoly capitalist bosses enforced their regime of intense exploitation by corrupting government and using political repression at the federal, state and local levels to deny workers their rights to organize, protest and strike for better wages and working conditions. Court injunctions, police, jails, law-and-order committees and even the hangman's noose were used at will by the monopolies to break strikes and deny workers their inalienable democratic right to organize and protest against their oppression as a class.

Yet the workers, Black and white, in the North and South continued to organize and fight back. As we have stated above, the Civil War ushered in monopoly capitalism/imperialism which forced workers to react rapidly and steadfastly to the new conditions as an independent class force. In the 1867 edition of *Capital, Volume 1*, Marx wrote: "But out of the death of slavery a new and vigorous life sprang. The first fruit of the Civil War was an agitation for the eight-hour day—a movement which ran with express speed from the Atlantic to the Pacific, from New England to California." [4]

"A movement for the eight-hour day," says Howard Zinn, "began among working people after the war, helped by the formation of the first national federation of unions, the National Labor Union. A three-month strike of 100,000 workers in New York won the eight-hour day, and at a victory celebration in June 1872, 150,000 workers paraded through the city."[5]

---

3   Foster, *The Negro People*, 389.
4   Marx, *Capital: Volume I.*
5   Zinn, *A People's History*, 354.

Outstanding leaders in the struggle for an eight-hour day were the German emigres who formed the first Communist Club of New York. They brought with them an understanding of scientific socialism and were especially active in the abolition movement prior to the Civil War, some of them (for example, Herman Meyer in Alabama and Adolph Douai in Texas) settling in the deep South to vigorously agitate against slavery. And there was of course Joseph Weydemeyer, close comrade of Karl Marx, founder of the first Communist Club in America, and a general in the Union Army. These class-conscious German workers not only participated in the abolitionist movement, but they waged a principled fight within the trade union movement on the question of equal rights for Black workers. They fought diligently to spread ideas of trade unionism and socialism among Black workers and other nationalities.

On September 13, 1871, some 20,000 workers marched in New York City for an eight-hour working day. The red flag of the First International was carried inscribed with the slogan "Workers of All Countries Unite!" As the procession toward city hall advanced, marchers were greeted with cries of "Long live the Paris Commune." When they arrived at city hall joined by 5,000 additional workers, the Black workers in the march were greeted with thunderous applause.

A few months later, on December 18, 1871 a company of Black soldiers known as the Skidmore Guard participated in a protest against the execution of leading Parisian Communards called by the International.

The International Workingmen's Association (IWA) sections in Chicago and other cities also carried on activities among the Black population. In Washington, D.C., Richard Hinton, who had taken part in John Brown's uprising at Harper's Ferry, is reputed to have been among the most active members of the Washington Section of IWA.[6]

These were remarkable advances unleashed no doubt by the democratic revolution taking place in the South in response to the pressing and immediate needs of the struggle for Black Liberation. But revolution also produces counter-revolution and the harbinger of the counter-revolution was the fact that the government, as we've stated previously, had refused to enact laws confiscating the vast estates of the slave holders. After the Civil War, the government did not break up land monopolies and these former slaveholders refused to even sell land, implements or farm animals to Black folk at any price. In the South, agrarian workers averaged about $60 a year in wages yet there was sufficient free land to easily grant a lot

---

6   Timothy Messer-Kruse, Yankee International: Marxism and the American Reform Tradition (University of North Carolina Press, 1998), 62

of 40 acres to every former slave. Meanwhile large land grants were being given to railroads and corporations.

The attitude of the communist members of the IWA regarding the urgency of the most pressing demands of the Black Liberation movement were not adopted by the labor movement as a whole. The new relationship of class forces in the wake of the Civil War and the rapid rise of monopoly capitalists made possible the defeat of attempts at Black and white unity led by the most advanced class-conscious workers. Between 1880 and 1890 the monopolists focused on corrupting the top leadership of the labor movement. The craft unions that dominated the American Federation of Labor were recruited into the service of the capitalist bosses to become strikebreakers, to prevent the organizing of the unorganized, to fan the flames of racism and to prevent the organizing of unskilled workers, women workers, Black workers and the foreign-born. Organized labor took no stand against Jim Crow, assumed an anti-socialist posture and became a part of the Wall Street mechanism of imperialism.

Lynching of Black people in the South became a method of social control and an open terrorist weapon of political reaction. Historically, in the South, lynching has always been the result of the actual or perceived loss of white privilege and is associated with the re-imposition of white supremacy. In the Northeast and West lynching was used against U.S. and foreign-born workers to keep them from organizing unions for better pay and working conditions. The San Francisco Vigilance Movement often mounted mob violence against the Irish, Chinese and Mexican communities.

It has been documented that 4,075 racial terror lynchings of African Americans in Alabama, Arkansas, Florida, Georgia, Kentucky, Louisiana, Mississippi, North Carolina, South Carolina, Tennessee, Texas and Virginia occurred between 1877 and 1950—at least 800 more lynchings of Black people in these states than previously reported in the most comprehensive work done on lynching to date.[7]

Ida B. Wells, a founder of the NAACP and most fierce and courageous opponent of lynching, gives us a report from the front line of the battle she led against lynching:

> The alleged menace of universal suffrage having been avoided by the absolute suppression of the Negro vote, the spirit of mob murder should have been satisfied and the butchery of Negroes should have ceased. But

---

7   "Lynching in America: Confronting the Legacy of Racial Terror," Equal Justice Institute, accessed September 1, 2020, https://eji.org/reports/lynching-in-america/.

men, women, and children were the victims of murder by individuals and murder by mobs, just as they had been when killed at the demands of the "unwritten law" to prevent "Negro domination." Negroes were killed for disputing over terms of contracts with their employers. If a few barns were burned some colored man was killed to stop it. If a colored man resented the imposition of a white man and the two came to blows, the colored man had to die, either at the hands of the white man then and there or later at the hands of a mob that speedily gathered. If he showed a spirit of courageous manhood he was hanged for his pains, and the killing was justified by the declaration that he was a "saucy nigger." Colored women have been murdered because they refused to tell the mobs where relatives could be found for "lynching bees." Boys of fourteen years have been lynched by white representatives of American civilization. In fact, for all kinds of offenses—and, for no offenses—from murders to misdemeanors, men and women are put to death without judge or jury; so that, although the political excuse was no longer necessary, the wholesale murder of human beings went on just the same. A new name was given to the killings and a new excuse was invented for so doing.[8]

And so, Jim Crow, Black Codes and lynching as a matter of fact deliberately brought about a reign of terror that effectively deprived Black people of the right to vote and imprisoned them within a system of social and economic inequality enforced by racial segregation. The intensified exploitation of the workers and farmers, the massive expropriation and internment (on reservations) of the indigenous population, and the political disempowerment and re-enslavement of Black people as sharecroppers were the indispensable preconditions for the rise of the monopoly capitalists to embark upon the road of imperialism.

Figure 3 — Ida B. Wells

Also, the rise of the monopoly capitalists and their unholy alliance with the Jim Crow South saw the

---

8   Ida B. Wells, "Lynch Law in America", *The Arena 23*, no. 1, (January 1900), 15-24, accessed September 1, 2020, https://www.digitalhistory.uh.edu/disp_text-book.cfm?smtID=3&psid=1113.

decline of the First International in the late 1870s due to internal strife. The headquarters was moved to New York. The essence of the split was this: The Marxists led by Otto Weydemeyer (son of Joseph Weydemeyer) maintained that the struggle for socialism must be waged by participating in daily militant trade union struggles, revolutionary propaganda and political action. On the other hand, the right opportunist followers of Ferdinand Lassalle favored forming cooperatives as opposed to engaging in class struggle that addressed the immediate demands of the workers and the Black people's struggles for equality.

From 1876 to 1900 the Marxist socialists held the helm in the Socialist Labor Party and stood united with Black people in the South, participating in their most courageous efforts to stop the former slaveholders and monopoly capitalists from disfranchising and re-enslaving them.

The untimely demise of the First International and the rise of right opportunism solidified the failure of the socialist movement in America to see the special nature of the question of Black liberation. This was a fatal ideological flaw. Looking at Black people as simply members of the working class meant subordinating important questions—of the struggles for national liberation, against racism, against the Jim Crow system and lynching—to problems of the working class in general. Such an approach fits in perfectly with the class collaborationist program of the economist opportunists in the trade union movement.

These setbacks took place at a time when organized labor and Black people needed to be allies. These setbacks were premised on the failures of the socialist movement to develop a program of unconditional solidarity with the struggles of Black people against Jim Crow oppression and lynch terror.

5

Monopoly Capitalist Attempts
to Harness Black Liberation

At the same time that the labor movement was being compromised, and the socialist movement divided between class-struggle militants and right opportunists, and as Black people were being murdered by lynch mobs and denied their civil and constitutional rights, there emerged in the South, up from slavery, a great organizing genius and social engineer named Booker T. Washington. Born on April 5, 1856, he was probably the last of national Black leaders born into slavery, and from 1890 to 1900 he basked in the sunshine of monopoly capitalism and was pumped up as the dominant leader of Black people.

Perhaps the most noted, marked occasion of his entre upon the stage of history was the Atlanta Exposition, where he was asked by members of the white business community to speak as a representative of Black people. After acknowledging that Black people are one third of the population of the South and pointing out that any business enterprise striving for success cannot afford to "…disregard this element of our population…" he goes on to demonstrate how the two races can reconcile their differences and work for a mutually prosperous future. This is how he formulated the question of Black liberation:

> A ship lost at sea for many days suddenly sighted a friendly vessel. From the mast of the unfortunate vessel was seen a signal, "Water, water; we die of thirst!" The answer from the friendly vessel at once came back, "Cast down your bucket where you are." A second time the signal, "Water, water; send us water!" ran up from the distressed vessel, and was answered, "Cast down your bucket where you are." And a third and fourth signal for water was answered, "Cast down your bucket where you are." The captain of the distressed vessel, at last heeding the injunction, cast down his bucket, and it came up full of fresh, sparkling water from the mouth of the Amazon River. To those of my race who depend on

bettering their condition in a foreign land or who underestimate the importance of cultivating friendly relations with the Southern white man, who is their next-door neighbor, I would say: "Cast down your bucket where you are"—cast it down in making friends in every manly way of the people of all races by whom we are surrounded.

Cast it down in agriculture, mechanics, in commerce, in domestic service, and in the professions. And in this connection it is well to bear in mind that whatever other sins the South may be called to bear, when it comes to business, pure and simple, it is in the South that the Negro is given a man's chance in the commercial world, and in nothing is this Exposition more eloquent than in emphasizing this chance. Our greatest danger is that in the great leap from slavery to freedom we may overlook the fact that the masses of us are to live by the productions of our hands, and fail to keep in mind that we shall prosper in proportion as we learn to dignify and glorify common labor and put brains and skill into the common occupations of life; shall prosper in proportion as we learn to draw the line between the superficial and the substantial, the ornamental gewgaws of life and the useful. No race can prosper till it learns that there is as much dignity in tilling a field as in writing a poem. It is at the bottom of life we must begin, and not at the top. Nor should we permit our grievances to overshadow our opportunities.[1]

The essence of Washington's philosophy was to assure capitalists that if they invested in institutions, like the Tuskegee Institute, to vocationally train Black people in bricklaying, blacksmithing, farming, etc., that this more than any other possible measure of reform would help Black people most of all in becoming accommodated to racial segregation as opposed to fighting it. He said, "In all things that are purely social we shall be as separate as the fingers, yet one as the hand in all things essential to mutual progress." He considered agitation for social equality an "extremist folly." No wonder Washington became personal friends with H. H. Rogers of Standard Oil and William Baldwin, vice president of Southern Railway and was idolized in grand bourgeois circles. No wonder President Theodore Roosevelt had him as a guest in the White House.

Washington represented small Black businesses and an aspiring Black bourgeoisie that sought a purely economic solution to the oppression of Black people. Harry Haywood describes it best when he says Washington was

---

1   Booker T. Washington, *Up From Slavery: An Autobiography*, (Doubleday, Page & Company, 1907), 219-220.

...definitely the voice of the embryonic Negro middle class which though staggered by the shock of the Hayes-Tilden sell-out, was again striving to reform its scattered ranks to break through to a place in the sun. Booker T. Washington's philosophy became its rallying point. Considering the times, the program of the sage of Tuskegee was by no means wholly negative...The inherent fallacy in the Washington doctrine was its compromising of the Negro's participation in politics to his economic rehabilitation....[2]

Let us quickly add that this "inherent fallacy" was fatal for the fight for social equality and against lynching.

Haywood was implicitly acknowledging that Washington represented an awakening national consciousness among Black people of the South. It was a national consciousness that rose out of a common oppression of an entire people; it was also a national consciousness driven by the narrow class aims of the Black bourgeoisie, as opposed to Black workers and farmers and the basic democratic demands of the Black masses who clearly wanted equality, land reform and their full citizenship rights.

But W.E.B. Du Bois, representing a progressive section of the emerging Black bourgeoisie, saw a triple paradox in

Figure 4 — Harry Haywood

Washington's philosophy. First, striving to promote Black businesses and property owners was not a bad idea per se, but impossible to pursue in the absence of voting rights and social equality. Second, how can Black people be self-respecting if at the same time they refuse to protest the civic inferiority imposed on them by draconian Black Codes and racist segregation? And third, how can you carry out a program of industrial training or vocational education without teachers trained in Black colleges or Black college graduates?

The reaction to these paradoxes came first from those Black folks who, in the tradition of Demark Vesey, Harriet Tubman, Nat Turner and other rebels, were agitated into action by the horrors of slavery. Driven by attitudes of revenge, hate and distrust they believed their only hope lay beyond

---

2   Harry Haywood, *Negro Liberation*, (Liberator Press, 1972), 172.

the borders of the United States. Perhaps Black people should seek refuge in Haiti or Africa. But given the reality that U.S. imperialism was now busy subjugating dark peoples in other lands, these emigration schemes fall apart as quickly as they are put together. The grandest example of this approach was the movement led by Marcus Garvey called the Universal Negro Improvement Association.

The second reaction came from the Black intelligentsia represented by individuals like Kelly Miller, J.W. Bowen and others. They could no longer remain silent. Their awareness of the social savagery perpetrated against Black people by the old Southern planter class in alliance with big business in the North compelled them, in good conscience, to put forth a simple program of demanding at minimum the right to vote, civic equality and the education of youth according to ability. In putting forth this program they refused to challenge the leadership of Washington; instead they sought a compromise—while agreeing that reasonable restrictions could be placed on voting so long as it also applied to white men and that the ignorance and degradation of Black people plays a role in their being discriminated against, still they said it is common knowledge that "relentless color prejudice is more often a cause than a result of the Negro's degradation."[3]

Du Bois mocked this tongue-in-cheek opposition to the Tuskegee Program and Washington's philosophy and accused these intellectuals of failing to state plainly the demands of the Black Liberation movement. His polemics were sharp and went to the heart of the matter:

> It is wrong to encourage a man or a people in evil doing; it is wrong to aid and abet a national crime simply because it is unpopular not to do so. The growing spirit of kindliness and reconciliation between the North and South after the frightful difference of a generation ago ought to be a source of deep congratulation to all, and especially to those whose mistreatment caused the war; but if that reconciliation is to be marked by the industrial slavery and civic death of those same black men, with permanent legislation into a position of inferiority, then those black men, if they are really men, are called upon by every consideration of patriotism and loyalty to oppose such a course by all civilized methods, even though such opposition involves disagreement with Mr. Booker T. Washington. We have no right to sit silently by while the inevitable seeds are sown for a harvest of disaster to our children, black and white.[4]

---

3   W.E.B Du Bois, *Souls of Black Folk*, (Taylor & Francis, 2015), 29.
4   Du Bois, *Souls of Black Folk*, 30.

Booker T. Washington may have been the darling of the imperialists but his allegiance to them did not stem the tide of Black resistance to the lynching and gaping social inequality that plagued the nation. Even before the NAACP was founded in 1909, Black people participated in the Anti-Imperialist League formed in Chicago in 1899. They opposed the imperialist war in the Philippines. *The American Citizen,* a Black newspaper in Kansas City, declared that imperialist expansion "means extension of race hate and cruelty, barbarous lynching and gross injustice to dark people." *The Broad Ax,* another Black newspaper called for a "National Negro, Anti-imperialist, Anti-trust, Anti-lynching League."

Under the leadership of Ida B. Wells and W.E.B. Du Bois, the NAACP (although in its inception it was largely white) emerged as the principal mass organization of Black and white people opposed to lynching and fighting for voting rights and social equality. After the lynching of a Black man in Coatesville, Pennsylvania in 1911 Du Bois cried out to the Black nation: "Let every Black American gird up his loins. The great day is coming. We have crawled and pleaded for justice and we have been cheerfully spit upon and murdered and burned. We will not endure it forever. If we are to die, in God's name let us perish like men and not like bales of hay."[5]

The end of the 19th century marked the end of the "old colonialism," economically rooted in the exportation of commodities as the foundation of the world market. And the beginning of the 20th century marked the dramatic arrival of imperialism economically rooted in the exportation of capital as the foundation of the world market. By now the export of surplus capital to developing countries or colonies had reached enormous proportions. "Typical of the old capitalism, when free competition held undivided sway," said Lenin, "was the export of goods. Typical of the latest stage of capitalism, when monopolies rule, is the export of capital."[6]

In the context of this development of imperialism it is not merely co-incidental that Sylvester Williams, a West Indian barrister, called the first Pan African meeting in London, England in this opening year of a new century. For the very first time in history the opponents of racism and imperialism met to discuss their common problems and engage the people of the world in the plight of Africans whose oppression was clearly the consequence of slavery and European colonialism. One of the two committees

---

5   Foster, *The Negro People,* 423.
6   Lenin, "Imperialism, the Highest Stage of Capitalism," in *Selected Works,* accessed September 7, 2020, https://www.marxists.org/archive/lenin/works/1916/imp-hsc/ch04.htm.

formed was chaired by W.E.B. Du Bois, who drafted an address "To the Nations of the World." The address opens with these historic words:

> In the metropolis of the modern world, in this the closing year of the nineteenth century, there has been assembled a congress of men and women of African blood, to deliberate solemnly upon the present situation and outlook of the darker races of mankind. The problem of the twentieth century is the problem of the color line, the question as to how far differences of race—which show themselves chiefly in the color of the skin and the texture of the hair—will hereafter be made the basis of denying to over half the world the right of sharing to utmost ability the opportunities and privileges of modern civilization.[7]

7   '(1900) W.E.B. Du Bois, "To the Nations of the World,'" *Black Past*, accessed September 7, 2020, https://www.blackpast.org/african-american-history/1900-w-e-b-du-bois-nations-world/.

6

The Color Line/Colonial Problem, World War and the Bolshevik Revolution

Coming out of the 19th century in the wake of Jim Crow and the rise of the U.S. imperialism, the country was approaching the 50th anniversary of the Emancipation Proclamation. The year was 1913 and Black people were feeling the need to soberly take stock of their situation. Progress had been registered mainly in terms of the Black Liberation movement taking on the character of a national movement with ties to a developing anti-imperialist movement.

The first challenge was the outbreak of World War I and revolution in Russia.

World War I was an imperialist war over re-dividing the world between the European colonial powers. Lenin declared: "…the Great Powers are waging an imperialist, capitalist war, a predatory war, a war for the oppression of small and foreign nations, a war for the sake of the profits of the capitalists."[1] Thus phrases such as "defense of the fatherland" are "capitalist deception."

The colonial looters, however, were describing this war as the war to end all wars and to make the world safe for democracy. Not appreciating the true criminal intent of the imperialists, some Black leaders like W.E.B. Du Bois (even though he wrote an essay on the "African Roots of War") encouraged Black people to participate in the war with a program of war-time demands to stop lynching and end Jim Crow laws. The following wartime demands were articulated by the NAACP:

> The right to serve our country on the battle field and to receive training for such service; (2) the right of our best men to lead troops of their own

---

1   V. I. Lenin, "Speech Delivered at an International Meeting in Berne, February 8, 1916," in *Collected Works*, vol. 22, accessed September 16, 2020, https://www.marxists.org/archive/lenin/works/1916/feb/08.htm#fwV22E031.

race in battle, and to receive officer training in preparation for such leadership; (3) the immediate stoppage of lynching; (4) the right to vote for both men and women; (5) universal and free common school training; (6) the abolition of Jim Crow cars; (7) the repeal of Jim Crow laws; (8) equal civil rights in all public institutions and movements.[2]

Unlike Du Bois, A. Phillip Randolph and Chandler Owen, editors of the *Messenger* magazine, joined Eugene Debs of the Socialist Party in opposing the war. "No intelligent Negro," said Owen and Randolph, "is willing to lay down his life for the United States as it now exists. Intelligent Negroes have now reached the point where their support of the country is conditional."

A Word about Lenin and the Russian Revolution

Just three years into the war a revolution led by communists triumphed in Russia. It sent shock waves around the world. For the first time since the Paris Commune, the workers rose to overthrow a capitalist government and to establish the dictatorship of the proletariat.

As Marxist-Leninists we are convinced that Vladimir Lenin played a key role in reviving the revolutionary content of Marxism and building a communist party of a new type, capable of bringing about the revolutionary overthrow of the old capitalist order. Stalin defined Leninism as Marxism in the era of imperialism and proletarian revolution, an era where socialism becomes an "immediate practical inevitability."

What is of the utmost importance is how Lenin further developed Marxism, making it the theoretical and practical foundation of the proletarian revolution during the revolutionary period 1905-1917. This could not have been done without Lenin and his comrades clashing with the opportunism of the Second International, with its class collaboration and national chauvinism (propped up by racist attitudes). Carrying out this task of relentless ideological struggle against the Second International was a necessary precondition for building a revolutionary vanguard party of the proletariat, the oppressed people in the colonies and oppressed nations held in bondage by the high-finance robber barons of imperialism.

Lenin's two great contributions to the further development of Marxism in the era of imperialism were: 1) To re-establish (in opposition to the revisionist-opportunists of the Second International) the fundamental

---

2   Foster, *The Negro People*, 432.

principles of Marxism as it was expounded and practiced by Marx and Engels. And 2) adding the lessons of the Bolshevik Revolution (See Lenin's *State and Revolution*) to developing a complete theory of socialist revolution and national liberation. Thus, Lenin unshackled Marxism from the opportunist revisionism of the misleaders of socialism by demonstrating in theory and practice that until the violent repression and resistance to the democratic struggles of the masses by the capitalist state and its backers is smashed and the dictatorship of the proletariat is established, socialism cannot be brought into being. Capitalism cannot be gradually reformed; it must be revolutionarily overthrown.

William Z. Foster wrote:

> Lenin, along with Stalin, developed the theory of colonial and national liberation revolution. He likewise demonstrated the basic need for cooperation between the colonial peoples and the revolutionary proletariat of the imperialist countries. Repudiating the entire body of Social-Democratic revisionist theory, Lenin also showed the revolutionary potentialities of the peasantry in alliance with and under the general leadership of the proletariat. Lenin, who was as great a strategist and tactician as he was a theoretician, developed the role of partial demands, of trade unionism, and of parliamentary struggle, thus solving many difficult problems of methods and weapons in the general fight of the working class for socialism. Lenin, throughout his entire work, thoroughly unmasked the opportunist Social-Democrats, showing them to be wedded to the capitalist system, and exposing the economic and political reasons why this was so.[3]

We have already mentioned the conditions of imperialism that emerged right before and during the Spanish American War of 1898. It is precisely those conditions, in part, that gave rise to Leninism. Lenin developed Marxism by rigorously demonstrating in his work *Imperialism, the Highest Stage of Capitalism* that the basic contradictions of capitalism had reached an extreme point, therefore, making proletarian revolution an immediate practical question.

For Lenin, imperialism meant capitalism at the point of death, the point of no return, the extreme limit where the old order ends, and revolution begins. The contradiction between capital and labor is still the driving force of capitalist development. However, when imperialism establishes the absolute power of the monopolies, banks and the whole financial oligarchy, it brings into being conditions where the ruling classes can no

---

3   Foster, *History of the Communist Party*, 50.

longer rule in the old ways of bourgeois democracy and where the "customary methods" of working-class struggles—like trade unions, cooperatives and parliamentary politics—are totally bankrupt if made an end in themselves. Imperialism by its very nature ushers in the era of revolution.

The driving force of revolution in the age of imperialism becomes the contradiction between a handful of so-called "civilized" nations and most of humanity (the so-called colored people) in the colonized and dependent developing countries. In these countries the imperialists squeeze out super-profits by exploiting labor to build railroads, factories, mills and mines and creating a native working class to work in these factories, mills, etc. New centers of commerce develop with an indigenous intelligentsia, an awakening national consciousness and inevitably a national liberation movement. And so, according to Lenin, this is how monopoly capitalism digs its own grave.

The proletarian revolution broke out in Russia not only because this is where all the contradictions of imperialism met, but this was also where all these contradictions expressed themselves in some of their most inhumane and barbarous forms.

Stalin put it succinctly in the following words: "Tsarism was the concentration of the worst features of imperialism, raised to a high pitch."[4] All these contradictions of imperialism in Russia made it pregnant with revolution; it also afforded the emerging Communist Party the unique opportunity of solving these contradictions in a revolutionary way.

The collapse of the Second International and the victory of the Russian revolution had a staggering and liberating effect upon the entire human race, but nothing quite matches the impact it had on oppressed nations in Africa, Asia and the Americas. In one revolutionary sweep, the Bolsheviks of Russia were seen all across the globe, in oppressor and oppressed nations alike, as the champions of the workers, the toilers of the land in the colonies and the racially oppressed. Lenin spoke with unmistakable clarity:

> The proletariat of the oppressor nations must not confine themselves to general, stereotyped phrases against annexation and in favor of the equality of nations in general, such as any pacifist bourgeois will repeat. The proletariat cannot remain silent on the frontiers of a state founded on national oppression; a question so 'unpleasant' for the imperialist bourgeoisie. The proletariat must struggle against the enforced retention of oppressed nations within the bounds of the given state, which means they must fight for self-determination. The proletariat must demand

---

4   Joseph Stalin, *The Foundations of Leninism*, (Foreign Languages Press, 1965), 7.

freedom of political separation for the colonies and nations oppressed by 'their own' nation. Otherwise, the internationalism of the proletariat would be nothing but empty words...[5]

Once the Third International (also called the Comintern) was convened in 1919 they took a clear, principled stand on the question of Black liberation. They declared,

> The Negro workers in America are exploited and oppressed more ruthlessly than any other group. The history of the Southern Negro is the history of a reign of terror—of persecution, rape and murder...Because of the anti-Negro policies of organized labor, the Negro has despaired of aid from this source, and he has either been driven into the camp of labor's enemies or has been compelled to develop purely racial organizations which seek purely racial aims. The Workers Party will support the Negroes in their struggle for Liberation, and will help them in their fight for economic, political and social equality...Its task will be to destroy altogether the barrier of race prejudice that has been used to keep apart the Black and white workers and bind them into a solid union of revolutionary forces for the overthrow of our common enemy.[6]

Here is the statement that goes to the crux of the matter: "The Workers Party will support the Negroes in their struggle for Liberation, and will help them in their fight for economic, political and social equality." Here the Communist International is not engaging in theoretical posturing but is making a declaration of unconditional solidarity with the Black Liberation movement.

Therefore, the Russian Revolution from day one entered upon the world stage extending the hand of unconditional solidarity to Black people in the United States and oppressed people everywhere living under imperialist domination. At the same time, the Communist Party, under Lenin's leadership, did not linger long before declaring itself on the "Negro Question." First there was intense discussion on the strategic importance of the Black Liberation movement and the need to do party work among Black people. Then in 1922 the Fourth Congress of the Comintern adopted the

---

5   V. I. Lenin, "The Socialist Revolution and the Right of Nations to Self-Determination," in *Collected Works*, vol. 22, accessed September 16, 2020, https://www.marxists.org/archive/lenin/works/1916/jan/x01.htm.

6   Phillip Foner and James S. Allen, eds., *American Communism and Black Americans: A Documentary History*, 1919-1929 (Temple University Press, 1987).

National and Colonial Commission's "Theses on the Negro Question."
The theses declared:

> The Fourth Congress recognizes the necessity of supporting every form
> of the Negro movement which undermines or weakens capitalism, or
> hampers its further penetration.
>
> The Communist International will fight for the equality of the white
> and Black races, for equal wages and equal political and social rights.
>
> The Communist International will use every means at its disposal to
> force the trade unions to admit Back workers, or, where this right already
> exist on paper, to conduct special propaganda for the entry of Negroes
> into the unions. If this should prove impossible, the Communist Inter-
> national will organize the Negroes in trade unions of their own and use
> united front tactics to compel their admission.
>
> The Communist International will take steps immediately to con-
> vene a world Negro congress or conference.[7]

These four theses had an immediate impact on the program of the Workers' Party which would later be called the Communist Party in the United
States. They issued a statement from their 1922 convention which stated,
among other things: "The Workers' Party will seek to end the policy of
discrimination followed by the labor unions. It will endeavor to destroy
altogether the barriers of race prejudice that have been used to keep apart
the Black and white and weld them into a solid mass for the struggle
against the Capitalists who exploit them."[8] In our opinion this was a return
to the revolutionary essence of Marxism.

In the late 1920s the Communist International concluded that African
Americans constituted an oppressed nation within the borders of the U.S.,
but we must hasten to add that the idea of a separate state did not originate
in the Communist International. On the contrary, the idea of a separate
state, as we shall demonstrate shortly, originated in the struggles for Black
liberation (going back to the days of slavery) and developed out of the national consciousness of Black people.

The petit-bourgeois left-opportunists and the ruling class intelligentsia
make the same assumption, that the idea of a Black Nation was something
hatched in the Comintern and imposed on the Communist Party who in

7   Jane Degras, ed., *The Communist International, 1919-1943*, vol. 1, (Oxford Univer-
     sity Press, 1956), 401.
8   Foner and Allen, *American Communism and Black Americans*, 20.

turn imposed it on Black people.[9] For example, see *The American Negro in the Communist Party: House of Representatives Committee on Un-American Activities* where they talk about "…the Communist Party plan for a separate state for the American Negro."

Another example of this attitude can be found in Cedric Robinson's *Black Marxism: The Making of the Black Radical Tradition.* Robinson, after portraying the African Blood Brotherhood playing some marginal role in the Communist Party addressing the question of Black liberation goes on to say: "Still, the historical and theoretical antecedents of the American Communist Party's work among American Blacks and its eventual positions on Black nationalism were substantially drawn from the experiences of Russian revolutionists."[10]

When we discuss in greater depth below the national question as it applies to Black people in the United States, we will note with historical precision that the concept of a Black Nation comes from Black people and that it went through various phases of development in relation to the struggle for Black Liberation. The call for a separate state was a demand of the Black Liberation movement not a plan of the Communist Party.

Emerging Black Urban Proletariat Develops Class Consciousness

The end of World War I and the triumph of the communist-led revolution in Russia coincided with some deep and abiding changes in the Black population in the United States. The Great Migration of tens of thousands of Black people leaving the South and going North in search of jobs and attempting to escape from the nightmare of Jim Crow racist oppression reached its peak in 1915 but continued almost non-stop until 1960; that is after nearly 7 million migrated. During World War I and the time of the Russian Revolution, Black people were rapidly becoming urbanized proletarians and militant working-class warriors. The right-wing-led American Federation of Labor (AFL) tried to characterize the Black workers as "strike breakers" and "allies" of the capitalist bosses. This was simply not true, for many Black workers fleeing from the lynching and racist segregation of the New Solid South were definitely in a fighting mood. Phillip Foner writes,

---

9   House Committee on Un-American Activities, *The American Negro in the Communist Party*, (U.S. Government Printing Office, 1954), 3.
10   Robinson, *Black Marxism*, 219.

> Most Blacks...were through with pleading for 'even-handed justice.' In both the steel strike and the Chicago race riot a new mood was detected among the Blacks. Roger Baldwin found radicalism widespread among the Negro strike-breakers and not, as charged, as the result of 'Bolshevik agents.' 'I found,' he reported, 'no trace of red propaganda, but I found observations and conclusions expressed in as red terms as I have ever heard from a soap box agitator. It is obvious that conditions themselves produce radical thinking.'...[11]

It is true that the militant mood of Black workers had its origins in the objective social and economic conditions that greeted Black people as they moved into Northern cities. This new, emerging Black proletariat was hungry, poor, and despised, desperately seeking jobs and forced to live in wretched slums. But also, there were serious attempts to organize and fight back. With regard to fighting back there were two movements going on. One was the movement of radical, socialist-led workers groups like the Industrial Workers of the World (IWW) and later the Communist Party; and the other was the very significant fact that Black workers were organizing themselves into unions and joining the socialist movement on their own terms.

In 1913, just eight years after the Industrial Workers of the World was founded, it created the Marine Transport Industrial Union. They recruited many Black waterfront workers along the Atlantic Coast. In a manifesto issued in late 1913 the IWW declared, among other things, that:

> We shall build a union that will be a real hope for all workers on the waterfront, black and white, a real support in the hour of our need, and compel the respect and recognition of all society. Generally speaking we shall ourselves assume control of our industry and dictate the conditions.[12]

This was the declaration of the Industrial Workers of the World as it entered the struggle of the dock workers, the unorganized longshoremen in Philadelphia. The Black worker and IWW organizer who led this campaign was Benjamin Harrison Fletcher.

On May 13, 1913 the Marine Transport Worker's Local 3 called a strike. Local 3 had been organized by the IWW over the opposition of the International Longshoremen's Association (ILA) and the Philadelphia branch of the Socialist Party. The African Methodist Episcopal Church

---

11   Foner, *Organized Labor*, 147.
12   Foner, *Organized Labor*, 112.

expressed the attitude of the Black community of Philadelphia when it announced, "The IWW at least protects the colored man, which is more than I can say for the laws of this country."[13]

Several weeks after the strike was underway the *Public Ledger* wrote: "...upward of 3000 Italians, Poles, Slavs and colored men, who are employed as stevedores, gang men and haulers have tied up the shipping industry in this city." Led by the IWW, the Black and white strikers held the line, battled the police who were protecting the scabs and called out the mayor. In spite of the vicious acts of police repression, in spite of the law-and-order stance of Philadelphia's politicians and the shipping industry's declaration that it would never negotiate; in spite of all this, Black and white workers, united in struggle, carried the day and won a final settlement for union recognition, the right to bargain collectively and 35 cents an hour. Ben Fletcher, one of the many courageous leaders in this historic class battle wrote in *Solidarity* (the official newspaper of IWW) "Only after many unsuccessful attempts to use scabs, police gunman, bribery, race prejudice, etc., to break their ranks the shipping trust was forced to surrender to the solidarity of labor."[14]

Philadelphia-born Benjamin H. Fletcher became active in the IWW while working as a longshoreman, loading and unloading cargo ships. He joined the Socialist Party and the Industrial Workers of the World (nicknamed Wobblies) in 1912. Within a year Fletcher became a leader and speaker, earning the respect and praise of his fellow workers for his gifts as a powerful speaker and union organizer. He also received praise for his oratory style and arguments for overthrowing capitalism, the ultimate goal of the revolutionary socialist movement.

The Wobblies proved that Black and white workers united could overcome racial and national divisions by building class struggle unionism and standing in unconditional solidarity with the struggle for Black Liberation.

Other locals of the Marine Transport Workers were formed in the South, namely, in Galveston, New Orleans and Baltimore. These locals were largely Black, but the principle of full equality of Black and white workers was consistently maintained. The IWW was demonstrating in deeds and declarations that the fight against Jim Crow racism and divisive racist policies was the foundation of Black and white unity and key to bringing class consciousness into the trade union movement.

The most telling challenge to IWW organizing of the unorganized Black and white workers in the South was the Southern lumbering

---

13 Foner, *Organized Labor*, 113.
14 Foner, *Organized Labor*, 113.

industry. In 1910 more than half of the 262,000 workers in Southern lumbering were Black. Of course, Black workers were locked into the lowest-paid unskilled jobs with virtually no opportunity to rise. In this same year, of the estimated 7,958 Black workers in the sawmills and planing mills of Texas, 7,216 were laborers. There was no Black sawyer. The average wage was $7 to $9 per week but this was not take-home pay per se. After working 12 hours a day, workers were paid in "script" or "time checks" which were simply a substitute for legal tender that came in the form of paper, cardboard coin or metal tags. This "money" could only be spent at the company store or converted into real currency at face value and the company store provided this service at a discount rate of 5% to 30%. Prices in the company store were sometimes 29 to 50% higher than the same merchandise in the surrounding community. Black workers were quick to learn from these practices that slavery came in different forms and so these conditions made the choice for fighting for organized union resistance inevitable. Workers sympathetic to the IWW and the Socialist Party started setting up organizing committees for the Brotherhood of Timber Workers in Louisiana and this movement spread rapidly into Texas and Arkansas. The Brotherhood of Timber Workers' constitution allowed Black workers to join but they bowed to the system of Jim Crow allowing for "colored lodges." Still Black workers joined. The capitalist bosses counter-attacked by blacklisting about 7000 of the most active known members and then proceeding with a lockout.

More than 350 mills in three states were closed. The locked-out workers would be allowed to return to their jobs if they signed a "yellow dog contract" denouncing the union, if they took an oath not to join the Brotherhood of Timber Workers and if they pledged loyalty to the bosses. The attitude of the workers to this treachery was aptly expressed by one Black worker who said: "Only a low-life lickskillet would do such a thing... I would live on wild plants that grow in the hills before I would sign."[15]

The company's attempt failed to breach the unity of the Black and white workers because no Black member of the Brotherhood of Timber Workers went back to work and only a few scabs could be recruited. "By May 1912, the brotherhood had a membership of 20,000 to 25,000 workers, about half of them Negroes."[16]

Despite these advances, these unprecedented acts of solidarity, the Brotherhood had not joined the IWW. Given the substantial number of Black workers in the Brotherhood of Timber Workers there was no

15   Foner, *Organized Labor*, 115.
16   Foner, *Organized Labor*, 115.

prospect of joining the American Federation of Labor with its capitulation to Jim Crow practices. So, it was decided by the leadership of IWW and the Brotherhood of Timber Workers to affiliate at the brotherhood convention to be held in Alexandria, Louisiana, in May of 1912.

Big Bill Haywood, legendary leader of the Wobblies, attended this convention and, when he saw that Black and white workers were meeting in separate halls, he addressed the white workers in the following words:

> You work in the same mills together. Sometimes a black man and a white man chop down the same tree together. You are meeting in convention to discuss the conditions under which you labor. This can't be done intelligently by passing resolutions here and then sending them out to another room for the black man to act upon. Why not be sensible about this and call the Negroes into this convention? If it is against the law, this is one time the law should be broken.[17]

The Black workers were invited into the hall and it was this mixed gathering that adopted the proposal to affiliate with the Industrial Workers of the World.

Some of the greatest pages in the history of the labor movement were written during the organizing drive of the IWW, led by class-conscious workers both Black and white. Too often organizing drives are portrayed as white workers organizing Black workers. This is a one-sided view which distorts the dynamics of the situation. In the South, while white workers overcoming racial prejudice in favor of class solidarity was crucial, it was not the driving force of the fight for multi-racial, multi-national class struggle unionism. The driving force was the Black men and women themselves who came to the union, who refused to scab and fought diligently with great sacrifice. Also, it is from these class battlefields that Black workers joined the socialists and later the Communist Party.

Forced by Jim Crow practices in the labor movement, Black workers organized their own unions and developed their own approach to the struggle for socialism.

Black Workers Organize Independently in the Struggle for Unity

We have already shown that, prior to the Civil War, Black workers in free and slave states alike formed their own independent labor and trade

---

17 Foner, *Organized Labor*, 116.

organizations. For example, we talked about the New York African Society for Mutual Relief and the Association of Black Caulkers in Baltimore, Maryland.

We also noted previously that after the Civil War or during Reconstruction, Black workers were fighting for admission to existing trade unions while they were organizing their own separate unions. George Myers, a Baltimore caulker and a member of a shipbuilding company organized by Black workers advised: "...It is the duty of colored men to look after their rights in the labor market."[18]

Myers believed that the Black workers should also associate themselves with the newly-formed National Labor Union (NLU). Showing up at the NLU convention in 1860 were delegates from independent Black unions from the North and South. From the South there was Isaac Myers of the Colored Caulkers' Trade Union Society and Ignatius Gross, from the Colored Molders' Union Society. Delegates from Pennsylvania included Robert M. Adger and Peter P. Brown of the United Hod Carriers' and Laborers' Association of Pennsylvania, John H. Thomas and James Roanne of the United Carriers Union No. 2 of Philadelphia and Isaiah Weir of the Workingmen's Union of Philadelphia.

The message of the Black workers to the National Labor Union convention was clearly stated by Isaac Myers. Myers stated,

> American citizenship is a complete failure, if [the Negro] is proscribed from the workshops of this country—if any man cannot employ who he chooses and if he cannot work for any man whom he will. If citizenship means anything at all, it means the freedom of labor, as broad and as universal as the freedom of the ballot.[19]

To illustrate that Black workers were opposed to organizing unions based on race, Myers said, "We carry no prejudices. We are willing to forget the wrongs of yesterday and let the dead past bury its dead." Myers told the story of Black shipyard workers being forced out of their jobs by striking white workers. In response the Black workers organized a cooperative, raised $40,000 and bought a shipyard of their own in order to employ themselves. "And," Myers continued, "is that all? No. We gave employment to a large number of men of your race, without regard to their

---

18 Foner, *Organized Labor*, 24.
19 Foner, *Organized Labor*, 25.

political creed, and to the very same men who once sought to do us injury. So you see gentlemen, we have no prejudice."[20]

This forthright stand of Myers on the question of civil and political equality was obviously challenging organized labor to step up and be in solidarity with Black people's struggles against Jim Crow and lynching. To this very day the labor movement as a whole has not met this challenge. The reason then was not solely due to the mental attitude of white workers but is due in large part to ruling-class attacks on the class-conscious labor movement by means of blacklisting, lockouts, law-and-order committees, orchestrated mob violence, legal lynching and every other means of brutal repression fashioned by the monopoly capitalist bosses and their corrupt boot-licking politicians. The reason for this failure of the labor movement to meet this challenge today is that the trade unions are, for the most part, dominated by class-collaborationist policies.

In the 1860s, when chattel slavery was coming to an end and a national labor movement was emerging, the revolutionary Marxist wing of the socialist movement was fighting and making every attempt permitted by circumstances to get organized labor to develop a consistent program of class struggle unionism that would proceed on the basis of Black and white unity. When Black Reconstruction was proceeding in a revolutionary manner it had a tremendous impact on the labor movement and demonstrated that by whatever measure Black people and their allies advanced the struggle for democracy in the South, by that same measure the labor movement benefited. For a moment the Socialist Labor Party held the helm and there were some rapid advances in class-struggle unionism and the fight against racism, but with the overthrow of Reconstruction, the collapse of the First International and the crushing of the national workers' rebellion of 1877, we saw the fight for democracy slaughtered on the altar of the new industrial capitalism.

Then came the racist and political repression released by the rise of monopoly capitalism and imperialism. Already these industrial capitalists were exploiting the uneven development between the North and the South. Jim Crow and the concomitant development of the sharecropping system in the South produced an environment brutally hostile to organized labor, yet it was precisely in the South that the radical socialist-led IWW conducted some of its most militant campaigns from 1912 to 1920. The Wobblies instinctively understood that the South was the battleground for the future of organized labor. They realized that for every advance in class struggle unionism there had to be a determined fight against Jim Crow

---

20 Foner, *Organized Labor*, 25.

practices in the trade union movement and unconditional support for the demands of Black people for equal rights as citizens. While the subjective evaluation of the Wobblies was based on good class instincts and Marx's analysis (in some instances) in the 1860s and 70s, it did not factor in the new objective social relations created by the rocket-like rise of U.S. imperialism.

W.E.B. Du Bois duly noticed the changes brought about by imperialism. He points out that just when the modern industrial working class was rising and beginning to flex its political muscle in demanding a larger share of capitalist profits in the United States and Europe, millions of Black workers throughout the world were emancipated. At first it was assumed that this mass of "dark workers" would develop along the same path as the white workers. Black workers received partial enfranchisement, some education and the elementary rights of wage earners and property holders. However, before these meager offerings of bourgeois democracy could take root there was the dawning of the age of imperialism and then this is what happened:

> The new colonial theory transferred the reign of commercial privilege and extraordinary profit from the exploitation of the European working class to the exploitation of backward races under the domination of Europe. For the purpose of carrying out this idea the European and white American working class was practically invited to share in this new exploitation, and particularly were flattered by popular appeals to their inherent superiority...[21]

The leaders of the trade union movement (particularly those in the craft unions) were being force-fed the idea of becoming a junior partner in the exploitation and enslavement of the peoples of Africa, Asia, Latin America, the Pacific Islands and the islands of the seas.

The monopoly capitalists did not simply engage in persuading organized labor to engage in class collaboration instead of class struggle. In 1918 the Black radical socialist Ben Fletcher was arrested along with 165 white Wobblies on charges of sedition and having obstructed the war effort. Fletcher was indicted by a Chicago federal grand jury. His crime was not speaking out against the war but successfully organizing Black and white shipyard workers along the East Coast. Federal grand jury indictments were returned on Wobblies in Fresno, Sacramento, Wichita and Omaha. The Red Scare was on, the Palmer Raids were in full effect and

---

21   W.E.B. Du Bois, *The Negro*, (Cosimo, Inc., 2010), 141.

the government, allied with the monopoly capitalists, was hell bent on destroying the IWW or any semblance of militant class struggle unionism. Fletcher and 101 Wobblies were convicted and sentenced to up to 25 years.

The *Messenger* magazine, which described itself as the "Only Radical Negro Magazine in America," launched a campaign to free Ben Fletcher. W.E.B. Du Bois quickly joined the campaign calling for Fletcher's release, declaring, "We respect the Industrial Workers of the World as one of the social and political movements of modern times that draws no color line." But no Black leaders were more outspoken for Fletcher's freedom than A. Phillip Randolph and Chandler Owen, editors of the *Messenger*. In one of the several articles they ran on Fletcher's case it was stated: "Ben Fletcher is in Leavenworth [the federal prison] for principle—a principle which when adopted, will put all the Negro leaders out of their parasitical jobs. That principle is that to the workers belong the world."[22] Significant support also came from C.S. Golden of the International Association of Machinists and others.

On the other hand, in 1921 the Department of Justice issued its "Report on All Wartime Offenders Confined in Federal or State Penitentiaries," recommending that Ben Fletcher not be released because: "He was a Negro who had great influence with the colored stevedores, dock workers, firemen, and sailors, and materially assisted in building up the Marine Transport Workers Union which at the time of the indictment had become so strong that practically controlled all shipping on the Atlantic Coast."[23]

To fully understand the movement of Black workers before and during the Russian Revolution, one must look at the Black Liberation movement as a revolutionary movement in and of itself. It began with slavery, because Black people as a people believed that that they had an inalienable human right to overthrow institutionalized government-decreed slavery by any means necessary. No one articulates the sacred right of Black people to use revolutionary means to overthrow their oppressors better than Frederick Douglass. "…it can never be wrong," said Douglass, "for the imbruted and whip-scarred slaves, or their friends, to hunt, harass and even strike down

---

22 Peter Cole, *Ben Fletcher: The Life and Times of a Black Wobbly*, (Charles H. Kerr Publishing Company, 2007), 24.

23 Miscellaneous Political Records, Political Prisoners, Department of Justice Files, December 10, 1921, TAF/c2c, National Archives, Washington, D.C., as cited by Philip S. Foner, "The IWW and the Black Worker," *The Journal of Negro History* 55, no. 1 (1970): 45-64, accessed September 28, 2020.

the traffickers in human flesh."[24] The act of rebellion and resistance of the oppressed precedes and lays the basis for the development of the revolutionary consciousness of the Black proletariat.

The way that the IWW and the left wing of the socialist movement approached what they called "The Negro Question" was summed up in an appeal issued by the Lumber and Timber Workers in 1922, which said, "As far as the 'Negro question' goes it means simply this: Either the whites organize the Negroes, or the bosses will organize the Negroes against the whites."[25] But this only begins to address the problem because it is not a question of whites organizing Black people into the labor movement when there is already an existing labor movement among Black people going all the way back to the days of slavery. It is more a question of how do whites work in solidarity with Black workers who have developed their own trade union movement due to the Jim Crow practices within the labor movement? Trying to bring Black people into the labor movement (and the socialist movement) in the absence of standing in unconditional solidarity with them in the fight against Jim Crow racism was the principal contradiction that blocked the pathway to Black and white unity—and the solution to this seemingly perennial problem will come from the advanced class-conscious Black workers and the Third International, or Comintern.

In 1900 Rosa Luxemburg posed the question: "The fate of democracy is bound up, we have seen, with the fate of the labor movement. But does the development of democracy render superfluous or impossible a proletarian revolution, that is, the conquest of political power by the workers?"[26]

The Russian Revolution gave a resounding no to this question. The Manifesto of the Communist International of 1919 declared:

> The world is on the verge of a new era…Europe is in revolt. The masses of Asia are stirring uneasily. The workers of the world are seeing a new life and securing new courage. Out of the night of war is coming a new day… The epoch of the final, decisive struggle has come later than the apostles of the socialist revolution [Marx and Engels] had expected and hoped. But it has come.[27]

The year 1917 was a year of working-class rebellions all over Europe and America as well as a year of uprisings of the colonially oppressed in India,

---

24   Douglas, *Life and Times*, 312.

25   Foner, *Organized Labor*, 116.

26   Rosa Luxemburg, "Reform or Revolution," in *The Essential Rosa Luxemburg*, (Haymarket Books, 2008), 88.

27   Winston James, *Holding Aloft the Banner of Ethiopia*, (Verso Books, 2020), 164.

China and South Africa. World War I was weary with the slaughter of millions of workers so that the imperialists could re-divide the world, and the blatant bankruptcy and vaunted national chauvinism of the Second International was now exposed for all to see. Stalin clearly points out what the Bolshevik Revolution meant in the context of the collapse of social democracy and the proletarian conquest of state power:

> Formerly, the national question was usually confined to a narrow circle of questions, concerning, primarily, 'civilized' nationalities. The Irish, the Hungarians, the Poles, the Finns, the Serbs, and several other European nationalities-that was the circle of unequal peoples in whose destinies the leaders of the Second International were interested. The scores and hundreds of millions of Asiatic and African peoples who are suffering national oppression in its most savage and cruel form usually remained outside of their field of vision. They hesitated to put white and black, 'civilized' and 'uncivilized' on the same plane. Two or three meaningless, lukewarm resolutions, which carefully evaded the question of liberating the colonies-that was all the leaders of the Second International could boast of. Now we can say that this duplicity and half-heartedness in dealing with the national question has been brought to an end. Leninism laid bare this crying incongruity, broke down the wall between whites and blacks, between European and Asiatics, between the 'civilized' and 'uncivilized' slaves of imperialism, and thus linked the national question with the question of the colonies. The national question was thereby transformed from a particular and internal state problem into a general and international problem, into a world problem of emancipating the oppressed peoples in the dependent countries and colonies from the yoke of imperialism.[28]

The Bolshevik Revolution for the first time in history united the liberation movement in the colonies with the proletarian revolution. Thus, the Third International boldly took up the challenge of conducting a relentless and determined struggle against the dominant-nation chauvinism of the "socialists" of the ruling imperialist nations. The so-called socialists of the Second International in Europe and Japan did not want to fight the imperialist policies of their governments and/or stand in unconditional solidarity with the oppressed peoples in the colonies fighting for self-determination and liberation.

Black revolutionaries in the United States saw the importance of the course of the revolution in relation to Black liberation and the

---

28 Stalin, *Foundations*, 70-71.

international struggle for socialism and they were delighted by what they saw. The *Messenger* magazine in an editorial entitled "The March of Soviet Government" stated:

> Still it continues! The cosmic trend of Soviet government with ceaseless step claims another nation. Russia and Germany have yielded to its human touch and now Hungary joins the people's form of rule. Italy is standing upon a volcano. France is seething with social unrest. The triple alliance of Great Britain—the railroad, transport and mine workers— threaten to overthrow the economic and political bourbonism of 'Merry Old England.' The red tide of socialism sweeps on in America. South America is in the throes of revolution.[29]

Of course, only in Russia did the workers seize power and hold it under the dictatorship of the proletariat. In Germany the workers' rebellion was drowned in blood with the brutal murders of Rosa Luxemburg and Karl Liebknecht. And in America the so-called "red tide of socialism" was being pushed back by the Palmer Raids, mass arrests and other forms of government-orchestrated political repression.

A Note on Hubert Harrison, Socialism and the Garvey Movement

We want to acknowledge an ardent supporter of the Bolshevik Revolution who was also a leading light in the Harlem Renaissance.

Hubert Harrison, a young Black revolutionary, from the tiny island of Saint Croix in the Virgin Islands, resigned from the New York branch of the Socialist Party in May of 1914 and joined the IWW, which was led by Elizabeth Gurley Flynn and William "Big Bill" Haywood. Harrison was a worker with encyclopedic knowledge and a gifted orator who joined the IWW because of their principled and anti-racist commitment to working class unity. A.

Figure 5 — Hubert Harrison

---

29   James, *Holding Aloft*, 164.

Phillip Randolph once described Harrison as the "Father of Harlem Radicalism."[30]

Harrison also played a pioneering role in the publication of many of the Black radical journals during and right after World War I. For example, there was Randolph's and Owen's *Messenger*, Cyril Briggs' *Crusader*, Garvey's *Negro World*, Bridges' *Challenge*, Claude McKay's *Liberator* and W.A. Domingo's *Emancipator*. Harrison's *Voice* was the archway through which all others passed. Hodge Kirnon, a contemporary observer and participant in the Harlem Renaissance, has written that the *Voice* was "the first organ to express the new spirit of the Negro…the credit must go [to Harrison] for being the first militant apostle of the New Negro. He assisted in molding and directing this new spirit and its accompanying ideals into their most effective channels."[31] And one might quickly add that he did so while trying to dialectically balance two apparently contradictory trends in the movement for Black Liberation, namely revolutionary socialism and Garvey's Universal Negro Improvement Association (UNIA).

Politically, Harrison differed from such Black revolutionaries as Randolph, Owen, Domingo, Grace Campbell (the only woman member of the African Blood Brotherhood) and Briggs in that he not only advocated both revolutionary socialism and Black nationalism, but actively engaged in the Garvey movement as a member of UNIA. It is even said by Harrison's contemporaries that he was the first person in Harlem to offer Marcus Garvey a platform to speak from. Seemingly, for every Black radical in Harlem except Harrison, Garvey's "back to Africa movement" to build a Black nation was the opposite of a revolutionary socialist movement; in essence they considered it an abandonment of the struggle of Black Americans for equality and full citizenship rights.

Harrison was vigorous in his critique of capitalism and its horrific consequences for Black people. He was an enthusiastic supporter of the Bolshevik Revolution and he never gave up on scientific socialism founded by Karl Marx and Frederick Engels. But he did not see the Socialist Party consistently embracing the revolutionary content of Marxism on the question of the racist discrimination and national oppression visited upon Black people. In the pages of the *Negro World* (the official organ of the Universal Negro Improvement Association) Harrison took on the Socialist Party's capitulation to Jim Crow practices in the South and the racist rationalizations they used to justify their actions.

---

30 James, *Holding Aloft*, 123.
31 Hodge Kirnon, "Hubert Harrison: An Appreciation," *New York Amsterdam News*, January 4, 1925, quoted in James, *Holding Aloft*, 126.

In 1920 Harrison wrote a polemical editorial in *The Negro World* entitled "Race First Versus Class First." In this editorial he pointed out that the Socialist Party turns a blind eye to the color lines being drawn by its Southern members. Case in point was that the party remained silent when a leading spokeswoman of the party was prevented from speaking to Black people on socialism while they were in the same hall with white people. Yet perhaps the most telling example was when the Socialist Party refused to route Eugene V. Debs to the South while he was running for president of the United States because he refused to remain silent on the "race question."

Harrison not only made a point of inconsistencies to demonstrate that the Socialist Party did not practice what it preached; he also went to the heart of the matter by exposing the racist attitudes of the party. He cites from a document that came out of the Socialist Party's national convention. This report, signed by leading members of the party, said "Race feeling is not so much a result of social as of biological evolution...class consciousness must be learned but race consciousness is inborn...."[32]

After spelling out this total abandonment of scientific, Marxist principles on the "race question" Harrison then goes on to state why he is a Black nationalist. Referring to himself he wrote,

> The writer of these lines is also a Socialist, but he refuses in this crisis of the world's history to put either Socialism or your party above the call of his race. And he does this on the very grounds which you yourselves have given in the document quoted above. Also because he is not a fool....your record so far does not entitle you to the respect of us who can see all around the subject. We say Race first, because you have all along insisted on Race First and class after when you didn't need help.[33]

There could hardly be a more poignant or militant expression of the impatience of Black radicals with the hypocrisy of the Socialist Party and its betrayal of the revolutionary principles of Marxism. Whereas Marx and Engels and the First International was saying labor in a white skin cannot be free so long as it is branded and sold in a Black skin, the Socialist Party, dominated by revisionists and white chauvinists, was saying that labor in a white skin must be free first. As we have seen that the seeds of this betrayal of Marxism goes back to the fall of the First International and the rise of the revisionists in the socialist movement, led by Ferdinand LaSalle and

---

32 James, *Holding Aloft*, 127.
33 James, *Holding Aloft*, 127-128.

German Social Democrats like Bernstein, whose slogan might as well had been: Reform Forever, Revolution Never. Hence, in response to this giant step backward the radical socialist component of the Black Liberation movement pursued its own revolutionary program.

Figure 6 — Cyril Briggs

The more advanced radicals of Hubert Harrison's followers, namely the African Blood Brotherhood, with Grace Campbell, Cyril Briggs and others, took up the challenge. Some of the programmatic ideas and tactics they put forward were as follows: 1) a liberated race; 2) absolute race equality; 3) the fostering of racial self-respect; 4) organized and uncompromising opposition to the Ku Klux Klan; 5) a united Negro front with which to oppose the Klan; 6) industrial development along cooperative lines; 7) wages for Negro labor, shorter hours and better living conditions; 8) education of the race at all levels and methods, including forums, newspapers, etc.; 9) cooperation with other darker races; and 10) cooperation with the class-conscious white workers. This was their ten-point program even though they never called it that.

The African Blood Brotherhood considered itself nationalist in form but revolutionary in content, so they were straightforward in their call for a multiracial alliance of workers against the capitalist bosses. Here is how they placed the challenge to Black people:

> The Negro masses must get out of their minds the stupid idea that it is necessary for two groups to love each other before they enter into an alliance against their common enemy. Not love or hatred, but Identity of Interest at the Moment, dictates the tactics of practical people.[34]

One can't be a nationalist without the ideal of building a nation and one can't be a revolutionary without the political objective of throwing off the yoke of national oppression. Such was the attitude and position of the African Blood Brotherhood leadership. But they aspired to have a secret organization with a mass base. When they issued a Recruitment Call

34 James, *Holding Aloft*, 171.

advertisement through the pages of *The Crusader* in 1920 they claimed that over 1000 men and women, "red blooded Negro patriots" had already joined. The call declared: "Ethiopia Expects That Every Negro This Day Will Do His Duty!" A program statement was later published claiming that the ABB was the first Black secret organization in the Western world having as its sole primary purpose the liberation of Africa and the rest of the Negro world. It would have all the trappings of a secret organization with its initiation ceremony, oath taking, degrees, passwords, signs, etc. There were no stipulated membership dues, each member paid according to their ability to pay. The structure of the organization was only revealed in outline, but it was pointed out that under the rules of the organization, when the "Supreme Council" issued "instructions" they must be considered law by every member of the Brotherhood.

"Suggestions," although not law, were expected "to command at least respectful and careful consideration." A list of 16 suggestions were put forward covering everything from organizing literary clubs to buying Black (supporting Black businesses) and encouraging participation in the Universal Negro Improvement Association. However, it is significant that the first suggestion on this long list read: "Affiliate yourself with liberal, radical and labor movements. Don't mind being called "Bolsheviki" by the same people who call you "nigger." Such affiliation won't solve our problems, but it will help immensely."[35]

Cyril Briggs and Hubert Harrison were both revolutionary Black nationalists who saw Black people in the United States as a nation within a nation necessarily engaged in struggle for national liberation and socialism.

Hubert Harrison left the Garvey movement and he never joined the Communist Party. He died December 17, 1927. His untimely death was a tragic loss to the Black Liberation movement in America and what was perceived at that time to be the Negro world. He was preeminently a working-class intellectual who courageously defied Jim Crow and rejected the accommodation policies of Booker T. Washington and Garvey's capitulation to capitalism.

Cyril Briggs, Harry Haywood, Grace Campbell and others who were a part of Harrison's legacy did join the Communist Party, because under the leadership of Lenin and the Third International, the party took the position of unconditional solidarity with the struggle for Black Liberation. In other words, it was the Bolshevik Revolution and the support they got from the Comintern, not a sudden change of attitude in the white-dominated communist movement in the United States, that attracted Cyril

---

35   James, *Holding Aloft*, 171.

Briggs and others to the party. In 1921 the Crusader put forth this une-quivocal proposition:

> The surest way, then, in our opinion to achieve the salvation of the Negro is to combine the two most likely feasible propositions, viz.: salvation for all Negroes through the establishment of a strong stable independent Negro State (along the lines of our own race genius) in Africa and else-where: and salvation for all Negroes (as well as other oppressed people through the establishment of a Universal Socialist Co-operative com-monwealth).[36]

---

36   Harry Haywood, *Black Bolshevik: Autobiography of an Afro-American Communist,* (Liberator Press, 1978), 125.

7

The Contributions of Black Revolutionaries to the Communist International Are Deeply Rooted in the Historic Struggle for Black Liberation

Cyril Briggs, who led the African Blood Brotherhood into the Communist Party, prided himself on the fact that he never joined the Socialist Party precisely because of its compromises with racist institutions and its betrayal of the revolutionary content of Marxism. Briggs was born May 28, 1888 on the island of Nevis in the Caribbean. His mother was Black, and his father was a white overseer. He received a thoroughly colonial education and migrated to the United States on July 4, 1905. Arriving in New York City in turbulent times, he joined a growing community of radical West Indians in Harlem. Within ten years he was writing for *The Amsterdam News*, the primary newspaper of Harlem's Black community. What we want to take up here is the fact that specific contributions of Black revolutionaries to the Communist International's formulation on the "Negro Question" are deeply rooted in the struggle for Black Liberation and pre-date the Russian Revolution by almost a century.

We have already provided an historical and socio-political context in which the idea of a Black nation came about. First of all, Black people, kidnapped into slavery and forcibly imported and sold like any other cargo, came to America in chains. They came from many different tribes (and perhaps even from some declining nations) along the west coast of Africa with different religious practices and languages, but under whips, chains and the toils of slavery they were forced and forged into one oppressed people sharing a common territory. The rulers of the nation and the society they found themselves in told them they were enslaved because of the color of their skin and their being "uncivilized."

In the early days of slavery, let us say during the time of the Revolution of 1776 up to 1800, the question of freedom for African slaves was a nagging one. This was especially the case after the British were defeated and the 13 colonies were no longer the political vassals of King George III. In fact, during the Revolution some Black people went over to the side of the British because they were promised freedom. After the war many were freed by the British and some were even resettled in "Free Town" in West Africa's Sierra Leone, a settlement created by British abolitionists for freed African slaves.

The decisive factions of the bourgeois ruling class after the American Revolution were the Northern capitalist merchant class and the Southern slaveholders. The Northern bourgeoisie were not only merchandisers but transporters and bankers as well. They were responsible for some small manufacturing and the beginnings of a wage-earning working class mainly working as seamen, dockers, carters, day laborers, clerks and agricultural workers. The Southern slaveholding faction consisted mainly of white planters who were capitalist landlords that controlled and owned gangs of slaves who were ruthlessly exploited in cotton and tobacco production.

Looking at the Declaration of Independence, which was written in part by Thomas Jefferson (a slaveholder with democratic ideas) and issued from the home of a bricklayer, and which says, "All men are created equal" with "certain unalienable rights," one could easily conclude that this was a clarion call to the oppressed to take up arms against their oppressors. In fact, based on what it says, this Declaration asserts in no mistakable terms the right of the people to make revolution against tyrannical and unjust governments.

We know from a long and bitter historical experience that bourgeois-led national revolutions were, in their day and time, epoch-making victories for social progress and human freedom. At the same time, the Revolution of 1776 was basically a struggle over which bourgeoisie would control the market. Would it be the one in England or the one in America? The defeat of the British settled this question. Foster writes,

> The richest merchants and wealthiest planters set out essentially to create a United States in which, they acting jointly, would own land and the industries and completely control the government. The Negroes would remain slaves permanently and the white workers, deprived of the franchise and other civil rights, would be merely objects for unbridled capitalist exploitation. All this meant that the Revolution had entered a new stage—from primarily a national struggle against England, it was being transformed into a sharp class struggle on the domestic scene.[1]

---

1   Foster, *The Negro People*, 57.

The abolitionist movement had found its first expression in the democratic upsurge of the people that followed in the wake of the revolution and its first victory in the abolition of slavery in the northern and northwestern states and territories (at that time, Ohio west to the Mississippi River and north to the Canadian border, catching about a third of what is now Minnesota). Thomas Jefferson's Northwest Ordinance, which went into effect in 1787, abolished slavery only in the "Northwest." It provided in part that "There shall be neither slavery nor involuntary servitude in the said territory, otherwise than in the punishment of crimes, whereof the party shall have been duly convicted..." But the Northwest Ordinance did not go counter to the later-enacted Fugitive Slave Act; runaway slaves still had to be returned to their masters.

At once the reactionary alliance between the Northern merchant capitalist and Southern slaveholder planter set out to crush the peoples' democratic movement unleashed by the Revolution of 1776. They shamelessly manipulated the Constitutional Convention of 1787 to leave Black people, one of the driving forces of the democratic mass uprising, in bondage and to allow slaveholders representation in the national congress by counting slaves as $3/5^{th}$ of a human being. Later, Congress passed the Fugitive Slave Act of 1793. George Washington, the first president and a slaveholder, presided over this counter-revolutionary measure and his successor President John Adams continued this process with the passage of the Alien and Sedition Acts of 1798, which were designed to terrorize foreign-born workers and immigrants who might harbor revolutionary and/or abolitionist sentiments. This law was also aimed at vilifying the French Revolution and served those who portrayed the French revolutionaries as atheist, anarchist, communists, and destroyers of the home and "civilization as we know it."

Black people were held in bondage as chattel slaves in the South and systematically denied the rights of citizenship in the North. They could not vote, serve on juries or in the military. They were denied access to education and shut out of an extensive line of trades and occupations, condemned to the most menial jobs and kept out of every hotel, inn and tavern.

Black folk in the face of these outrages and as a way of fighting back formed their own institutions. In this context, the Black church took root and became one of the main sources and a component part of the Black Liberation movement. The churches were pioneers in the development of separate institutions and the national organizing of Black people. One might call this the embryonic stage of the Black Liberation movement, the gestation period, or the preliminary stages of the fetal development of Black people seeing themselves as an oppressed nation within a nation. This was the historical moment in which Bishop Richard Allen, Sarah Bass and Absalom Jones founded the African Methodist Episcopal (AME) church, the first national Black church. Sarah Bass, Richard Allen's wife, was appropriately called the mother of the first national Black church.

Figure 7 — Richard Allen

Figure 8 — Sarah Bass Allen

The formation of the AME nationally laid the foundation for the Colored Convention Movement. What first sparked free Black folk into having conventions was the creation of the American Colonization Society by the slaveholders to bring about the mass deportation of the free Black community back to Africa. This pro-slavery movement was designed to destroy the possibility of free Black people leading a militant, revolutionary abolitionist movement. Consequently, the earliest manifestation of the Colored Convention Movement occurred in 1817 when local conventions were organized to oppose the program of the American Colonization Society and to insist on their right to remain in the United States to fight for the liberation of their sisters and brothers who were still chattel slaves.

The first national Colored Convention was held September 1830 at Mother Bethel AME Church in Philadelphia. The main item on the agenda was emigrating to Canada. Due to the existence of fugitive slave laws, the convention discussed the idea of buying some land in Canada to create a refuge for free Black people and runaway slaves. It was decided to seek refuge in Canada and at the same time address the institutionalized racist practices (slavery in the South and racial discrimination in the North) that existed in the United States.

The emergence of the Colored Convention Movement was very important in the development of a national consciousness among Black people. It was a new beginning or turning point in that it started the process of institutionalizing the struggle for Black Liberation on a national and international level. The process consisted of having a series of national, regional and state conventions that organized and engaged every facet of the national community of Black folk. This fact was reflected in the attendance at these conventions: Black people free from slavery and those who were fugitive slaves, as well as abolitionists, businesspeople, writers and publishers. The Colored Conventions were organized with the objective of developing a program of liberation for those who were in bondage as chattel slaves and those who were not slaves but still denied citizenship rights and discriminated against. They demanded an end to slavery and racial discrimination and segregation. The key issues discussed and resolved concerned labor organizing, health care, educational equality and temperance.

The Colored Convention Movement was fostered by not only the AME churches but also by the appearance of Black newspapers like *Freedom's Journal* (1827-29) and later the *Colored American* (1837-41).

But there were many other pioneers in this early development of Black folk becoming conscious of themselves as a people entitled to their own sovereign existence. There was Prince Hall, the educator; Benjamin Banneker, the astronomer and mathematician; Phyllis Wheatley, the poet who was born in Senegal in west Africa; Jupiter Hammon, poet, freedom-fighter and abolitionist, and Paul Cuffee, born free in the state of Massachusetts, prominent in the New England shipping industry and a freedom-fighter and abolitionist.

From its earliest stages the Black Liberation movement has been characterized by the fight for equality and the right of Black folk to their own separate existence as a dignified people, free from the oppression imposed on them by the white ruling class in the South and the North. These two trends have often been contradictory but never mutually exclusive. For example, Martin R. Delany, who fought alongside such leading revolutionary abolitionists as Frederick Douglass and Harriet Tubman, was also the first to call for a separate Black nation on African soil. Looking at his development as a nationalist will deepen our understanding of the fact that Black nationalism as a movement is a direct response to a recalcitrant white ruling class and the aspirations of Black people to be free to determine their own political destiny. That is why in every phase or stage of the struggle for Black Liberation the question of self-determination arises both spontaneously and organizationally.

Figure 9 — Martin Robinson Delany

Before Cyril Briggs ever breathed a word about a separate Black nation there was Martin Robinson Delany. Delany was born May 6, 1812, the son of a free mother and an enslaved father. Under the slave laws of Virginia, he was born free. On his father's and mother's side his grandparents were born in West Africa. He was an accomplished writer and publisher who started his own newspaper, *Mystery*, in 1843 and later, around 1847, joined Frederick Douglass in editing and publishing the *North Star*. He apprenticed under several physicians and went on to practice medicine. He applied to attend various medical schools, including Harvard, but because he was Black, he was denied entry. Delany went on to become a brilliant organizer and champion of Black liberation.

Delany's views were set forth in his book, *The Condition, Elevation, Emigration, and Destiny of the Colored People of the United States, Politically Considered,* published in 1852, where he argued that Black people had no future in the United States. He thought they should leave the United States and found a new nation elsewhere, perhaps in the West Indies or South America. But what is even more important is how Delany advances this proposition.

Delany's book is the first book on the condition of Africans in America that offers a class and race analysis and puts forth a theoretical postulation on the question of Black liberation. Let us take a quick look at some of its main propositions.

Delany starts by offering an historical analysis of the struggle between oppressors and oppressed. He writes:

> That there have been in all ages and in all countries, in every quarter of the habitable globe, especially among those nations laying the greatest claim to civilization and enlightenment, classes of people who have been

deprived of equal privileges, political, religious and social, cannot be denied, and that this deprivation on the part of the ruling classes is cruel and unjust, is also equally true. Such classes have even been looked upon as inferior to their oppressors, and have ever been mainly the domestics and menials of society, doing the low offices and drudgery of those among whom they lived, moving about and existing by mere sufferance, having no rights nor privileges but those conceded by the common consent of their political superiors. These are historical facts that cannot be controverted, and therefore proclaim in tones more eloquently than thunder, the lustful attention of every oppressed man, woman, and child under the government of the people of the United States of America.[2]

After putting the question of the oppression of Black people in the context of the historic struggles between oppressor and oppressed, Delany then proceeds to discuss the national character of their oppression:

That there have in all ages, in almost every nation, existed a nation within a nation—a people who although forming a part and parcel of the population, yet were from force of circumstances, known by the peculiar position they occupied, forming in fact, by the deprivation of political equality with others, no part, and if any, but a restricted part of the body politic of such nations, is also true. Such then are the Poles in Russia, the Hungarians in Austria, the Scotch, Irish, and Welsh in the United Kingdom, and such also are the Jews, scattered throughout not only the length and breadth of Europe, but almost the habitable globe, maintaining their national characteristics, and looking forward in high hopes of seeing the day when they may return to their former national position of self-government and independence, let that be in whatever part of the habitable world it may. This is the lot of these various classes of people in Europe, and it is not our intention here, to discuss the justice or injustice of the causes that have contributed to their degradation, but simply to set forth the undeniable facts, which are as glaring as the rays of a noon-day's sun, thereby to impress them indelibly on the mind of every reader of this pamphlet.

Such then is the condition of various classes in Europe; yes, nations, for centuries within nations, even without the hope of redemption among those who oppress them. And however unfavorable their

---

2   Martin Robison Delany, *The Condition, Elevation, Emigration, and Destiny of the Colored People of the United States and Official Report of the Niger Valley Exploring Party*, (Humanity Books, 2008), 41.

condition, there is none more so than that of the colored people of the United States.[3]

The United States, according to Delany started out,

> ...untrue to her trust and unfaithful to her professed principles of republican equality, has also pursued a policy of political degradation to a large portion of her native born countrymen, and that class is the Colored People. Denied an equality not only of political but of natural rights, in common with the rest of our fellow citizens, there is no species of degradation to which we are not subject.[4]

It was not enough that the overwhelming majority of Black folk were forced to live in abject slavery but their descendants who were free and who lived outside the jurisdiction of the slave states were also denied, the same as slaves, their civil, religious and social privileges. Slave or free descendants of Africans were at the bottom of the social ladder. Driving this point home Delany cried out:

> In those States, the bondman is disfranchised, and for the most part so are we. He is denied all civil, religious, and social privileges, except such as he gets by mere sufferance, and so are we. They have no part nor lot in the government of the country, neither have we. They are ruled and governed without representation, existing as mere nonentities among the citizens, and excrescences on the body politic—a mere dreg in community, and so are we. Where then is our political superiority to the enslaved? none, neither are we superior in any other relation to society, except that we are defacto masters of ourselves and joint rulers of our own domestic household, while the bondman's self is claimed by another, and his relation to his family denied him. What the unfortunate classes are in Europe, such are we in the United States, which is folly to deny, insanity not to understand, blindness not to see, and surely now full time that our eyes were opened to these startling truths, which for ages have stared us full in the face.[5]

It was in this manner that Delany eloquently and forcefully set forth and examined the objective social relations and conditions that gave rise to the demand for a separate nation and the right to self-determination. His work

---

3   Delany, *The Condition, Elevation, Emigration, and Destiny of the Colored People*, 42-43.

4   Delany, *The Condition, Elevation, Emigration, and Destiny of the Colored People*, 44.

5   Delany, *The Condition, Elevation, Emigration, and Destiny of the Colored People*, 44.

proves that imbedded in the political consciousness of Black people is the idea of nationhood. This idea springs from the blood-soaked soil of oppression and it found expression in two powerful movements that Delany was a part of and helped to create, the Colored Convention Movement and the National Emigration Convention. Delaney presented the question of Black liberation to the National Emigration Convention in 1854 in no uncertain terms:

> ...no people can be free who themselves do not constitute an essential part of the ruling element of the country in which they live... The liberty of no man is secure, who controls not his own political destiny... A people, to be free, must necessarily be *their own rulers*... But we have fully discovered and comprehended the great political disease with which we are affected, the cause of its origin and continuance; and what is now left for us to do, is to discover and apply a sovereign remedy—a healing balm to a sorely diseased body—a wrecked but not entirely shattered system. We propose for this disease a remedy. That remedy is Emigration.[6]

The struggle for self-determination may take many forms, depending on the relationship of forces and the organized strength of the movement relative to the power of the oppressor. But the essence of what it means is the recognition of the sovereignty of a people in all matters affecting their internal life as well as in matters involving their relationships with other peoples or nations. These incudes the right to separation or independence. And there is no doubt that this principle was first articulated by Richard Allen, Sarah Bass, Martin R. Delany and others from 1830 to 1854.

This "Black Manifesto" of 1854 came out within six years of the opening shots of the Civil War. It came out during that most dismal moment in history, when the reactionary tide of the slaveholders was sweeping the land and the Supreme Court had declared that Black people had no rights that white people were bound to respect. It came out in that darkest hour before the dawn of the revolution that abolished chattel slavery.

All that we have stated above demonstrates that the idea of a separate Black nation had been nurtured in the Black Liberation movement from at least the early 19th century. When Cyril Briggs puts forth this same idea he is soundly rooted in the revolutionary traditions of Black people.

---

6   Martin Robison Delany, et al, "Political Destiny of the Colored Race, on the American Continent," *Proceedings of the National Emigration Convention of Colored People*, held at Cleveland, Ohio, August 24, 1854 (A. A. Anderson, 1854), 35-37, accessed October 22, 2020, https://omeka.coloredconventions.org/items/show/314.

The ideological development of the struggle for Black Liberation had been going on for a whole century when the proletarian-led Russian Revolution triumphed in 1917. Black people were starting to see themselves as an oppressed nation within a nation in 1817. Also, it is important to note that a conscious relationship between the socialist movement and the Black Liberation movement existed prior to the Russian Revolution and that class-conscious Black workers and revolutionary Black nationalists sought alliances with class-conscious white workers who rejected racist Jim Crow policies and were internationally minded socialist revolutionaries.

Before the Civil War, most Black people were slaves and, therefore, were forbidden by their masters to be a part of any organized political movement. During slavery, the Marxist socialists were the only socialists who were militant abolitionists. Robert Owen, a leading utopian socialist, said he had seen worse slavery in England than chattel slavery in the southern United States. And for this reason alone, he declared that he would "contend for the liberty of the white man, who was bound by the most arrant slavery of all."[7]

Peter H. Clark is the first Black American on record to publicly identify himself as a Marxist socialist. This occurred on March 26, 1877 when Clark announced his support of the Workingmen's Party of the United States, the first Marxist political party in this country.[8] However, as the First International morphed into the Second International there was to develop an ever-present bone of contention between the socialists in the Second International and the revolutionary leaders of the Black Liberation movement.

As we have previously stated, some Black revolutionaries such as Hubert Harrison and Cyril Briggs believed that the Socialist Party, in capitulating to racism, had betrayed the revolutionary essence of Marxism.

Cyril Briggs, Grace Campbell, Harry Haywood, Claude McKay and others saw in the Russian Revolution a radical shift in the international balance of power that favored the national liberation struggles against European colonialism in general and the struggle for Black Liberation in the United States in particular.

---

7   Phillip S. Foner, *Essays in Afro-American History*, (Temple University Press, 1978), 155.

8   Foner, *Essays in Afro-American History*, 154.

Figure 10 — Grace Campbell

"The Bolsheviks," writes Harry Haywood, "had destroyed the czarist rule, established the first workers' state, and breached the world system of capitalism over a territory comprising more than one-sixth of the earth's surface. Most impressive as far as Blacks were concerned was that the revolution had laid the basis for solving the national and racial questions on the basis of complete freedom for the numerous nations, colonial peoples, and minorities formerly oppressed by the czarist empire."[9]

Lenin's views on the National Question took into consideration how the rise of modern imperialism polarized the world into oppressed and oppressor nations. Marx said white workers could not be free while Black workers existed as chattel slaves. Only Black and white workers united can defeat the capitalist bosses. Lenin, updating Marx in the age of imperialism, said the white workers of Europe cannot be free while the great mass of humanity (being people of color) is enslaved and super-exploited in the colonies and oppressed nations by the imperialists.

At the Seventh International Socialist Congress of the Second International held in Stuttgart, Germany, in 1907, Lenin, leading the Bolshevik faction, called for an alliance between workers and peasants—an alliance between the proletariat of the advanced industrialized countries of the West and the predominantly peasant-based national revolutionary movements of the East. Lenin saw this alliance as the pathway to bringing about a socialist revolution and defeating imperialism. To be successful the revolutionary socialist movement must be consciously linked to the revolutionary national democratic and anti-colonial movements. In 1917 the Bolsheviks turned this proposition on the National Question into policies of the new revolutionary government. But not without considerable difficulties.

With regard to developing a sound policy on the question of Black liberation in the United States, John Reed wrote to Gregori Zinoviev on February 25, 1919 regarding the oppression of Black Americans and the growing militant fightback against lynching and other forms of violent repression. Reed pointed out that Black publications like the *Messenger* were

---

9   Haywood, *Black Bolshevik*, 118-119.

even preaching revolutionary socialism and that their ideological orienta-
tion was "semi-nationalist, semi-communist." Responding to Lenin's call
for unconditional solidarity with the nationally oppressed peoples of the
world, Reed also noted that Black Americans had developed "a strong racial and social movement" with a rapidly growing class consciousness. He
then went on to point out that Black people did not seek a separate national existence. Therefore, Black people should be viewed as a vital part
of the working class and brought into the labor movement. Communists
should argue the futility of bourgeois democracy and the necessity of socialist revolution because this is the only way to get rid of the burden of
racial oppression. Although garbed in revolutionary rhetoric, in essence
Reed's position was no different than the color-blind economism of the
Second International Social Democrats. Reed was still caught in the snares
of a one-dimensional class analysis that at its best could only grant that
Black people were racially oppressed. However, the principal ideological
flaw is Reed's denial of the reality of Black people seeing themselves as an
oppressed nation within a nation. Even at the time he made this assessment, the United Negro Improvement Association was rapidly becoming
the largest mass non-religious organization of Black people in the United
States.

Lenin's "Draft Theses on National and Colonial Questions For The
Second Congress Of The Communist International" carried the day at the
Second Congress where he urged communist parties to support "revolutionary movements among the dependent and underprivileged nations (for
example, Ireland, the American Negroes, etc.) and in the colonies."[10]
Clearly the Comintern had decided to break sharply with the social democrats by recognizing the special oppression of Black people in Africa and
America. Lenin's view, compared to Reed's view, was far more compatible
with the historically developed national consciousness of Black people in
the age of imperialism.

At the Fourth Congress in 1922 Black Americans showed up for this
first extensive discussion of the "Negro Question." It was a somewhat awk-
ward situation, with communist parties from the U.S. and South Africa
being overwhelmingly white. Naturally it was the Black Americans, led by
the militant and brilliant Claude McKay who stressed not only the special
character of racist and national oppression of Black people but also pointed
out the ideological capitulation of the party in dealing with racial prejudice.

---

10   V. I. Lenin, "Draft Theses on National and Colonial Questions For The Second
     Congress Of The Communist International," in *Collected Works*, accessed October
     24, 2020, https://www.marxists.org/archive/lenin/works/1920/jun/05.htm.

The 33-year-old McKay was supported by Harlem radicals in his desire to visit the cradle of the proletarian revolution. Among his supporters were James Weldon Johnson (author of the *Black National Anthem*), Richard B. Moore and Arthur Schomburg (Black Puerto Rican founder of the Schomberg Library in Harlem). With credentials from the African Blood Brotherhood, it was McKay who exposed the basic weaknesses of the Communist Party on the question of Black liberation and called for a "Negro Congress" so that the Comintern could see for itself the fine revolutionary potential and determination of Black people and "the fine material for communist work there is in the Negro race."

A Japanese revolutionary, Sen Katayama, head of the Eastern Section of the Comintern supported Claude McKay. Katayama strongly believed that Black voices needed to be heard by the Comintern, and it is through him that McKay got a pass to the Fourth Congress.

At any rate these new tendencies moving toward seeing Black people as an oppressed nation were formalized in a letter of instructions sent to the Workers Party by the Executive Committee of the Communist International in December 1924. This confidential communication from the ECCI proposed that communists call for an American Negro Labor Council and that: "The 'Right of Self-Determination even to Separation' must be complemented for America by the demands of absolute social equality."[11] This slogan at least recognized what Black people had been articulating since the Colored Convention Movement in 1830.

We will not offer here a detailed discussion of the intense ideological struggle that took place to arrive at this unequivocal demand for the destruction of Jim Crow in all areas of American life and especially in the trade union movement. (We do offer a detailed analysis later in this book and we use as our source the writings of Harry Haywood and original documents presented in *American Communism and Black Americans: A Documentary History, 1919-1929*, Temple University Press, Philadelphia 1987. Edited by Phillip S. Foner and James S. Allen.) We will not discuss how the Communist International squared the demand for absolute equality with their recognition of the right of Black workers to organize separate unions or organizations. Suffice it to say that once agreement was reached by the Executive Committee of the Communist International October 26, 1928 it had to be enforced through centralized guidance, i.e., move it from a dead letter to living practice. The Workers Party was instructed to dissolve its autonomous foreign-language federations and to consolidate the

---

11   Mark Solomon, *The Cry Was Unity: Communists and African Americans*, 1917-1936, (University Press of Mississippi, 1998), 48.

entire membership into neighborhood and shop units. The party would become multiracial and multinational at its base and in its leadership. This process was not an easy one, but it was a radical break with segregated practices and a grand entre upon the thorny road to Black and white unity in a society terrorized and dominated by racial/national, class and sexist oppression. The vehicle for bringing about this new united struggle would be the American Negro Labor Council (ANLC).

In this new reality of connecting party work with the masses of Black and white workers new antagonisms and contradictions came forth in the course of widening relationships with the people and fighting Jim Crow. It was not a perfect vehicle, but it was a progressive one, breaking ground where none had been broken before and challenging too-long endured racist practices. Substantial numbers of people of all races and nationalities, both men and women, and in particular young people new to the cause of revolution would be brought into the party as a result of the party taking up in practice the struggle against white chauvinism and the struggle for Black Liberation.

All propositions must stand the test of reality no matter how deeply they are rooted in past practice. The tension between "nationalism" and "class struggle" was being recognized by the Communist International, not resolved. This in and of itself laid the basis for a practical program of action that would take up the fight against Jim Crow and white chauvinism within the socialist movement. Comrade Sen Katayama, who was close to the American Black students in Moscow, made the following contribution, said he:

> As ably presented for the first time at the Congress, the Negro problems should be seriously considered and a policy decided upon for the immediate future. The Negro question was fully discussed at the II. Congress by comrade Lenin and the American delegates, and certain principles were laid down for this work, as the II Congress considered the Negro question to be of great importance. Comrade Lenin considered the American Negroes as a subject nation, placing them in the same category as Ireland. At this II Congress, the American Party was instructed to investigate the possibility of calling a Negro Congress, first in America, and then a World Negro Congress. The criminal neglect of the Negroes on the part of the American Party, as already pointed out by the Negro representatives, is solely due to the factional struggles...
>
> The American Party has never utilized these revolutionary factors for the advancement of the revolutionary movement. This was particularly marked when the Anti-Lynch Bill was before the Congress, which gave immeasurable possibilities for gaining national sympathy for the Negro

race. The American Party failed to utilize the occasion of the passing of this Bill for revolutionary propaganda in the country. This Bill passed the House, in spite of the solid opposition from the South, but the Senate shelved the question, where it is still lying. The Party should take up this Bill and utilize it for energetic propaganda against the white oppression and persecution of the Negroes.

Comrades! I spent twenty-six years in America as a worker and was connected with the American movement. I have a right therefore to regard the American Party as mine...Unless the American comrades liquidate their factional struggles the American Party will not develop into a mass party. Of course, you have to overcome the social prejudices and impediments to conduct Party work among the Negroes, but it is your duty to carry out the instructions of the Comintern. Increase the Negro membership and let them solve their own problems by themselves under the guidance of the Party.[12]

Finally, the challenge of restoring the revolutionary essence of Marxism was being taken up in revolutionary practice and as it came about, that practice demonstrated that true internationalism transcends racial and national boundaries. Black revolutionaries and those revolutionaries representing the colonized masses of Africa and Asia saluted the Bolshevik Revolution, for taking "workers of the world unite" as a battle cry from the traitors of the Second International and giving it new meaning and substance through the courageous work of the Comintern. The slogan "Workers of the world unite" was updated to reflect this development and the rise of imperialism, becoming "Workers and oppressed peoples of the world unite." It was the Bolsheviks who turned the new Soviet government to the task of being a center for the struggles for socialism and national liberation. The Russian Revolution of 1917 ushered in a new era and put an end to the ideological hegemony of white European chauvinism in the international communist movement.

The Resolution on the Black Liberation Question in the United States

What we have attempted to demonstrate here is based strictly on the historical evidence; we have presented here that the right and exercise of self-determination is inherent in the historic struggle for Black Liberation in the United States. The form that the struggle for self-determination takes in any given moment of history is determined in the final analysis by the

---

12 Foner and Allen, *American Communism*, 188-189.

objective social relations, not by subjective evaluation. During the period of chattel slavery, the principal forms of struggle were the movement for the abolition of slavery and the Colored Convention movement. During Reconstruction it was the franchise, full citizenship rights and self-government in those geographical areas where Black people were a majority. The minimum requirements for self-government were the rights to vote (i.e. universal manhood suffrage) and hold public office.

Reconstruction became a period of revolutionary struggle for democracy and bloody counter-revolution because Black-controlled governments in the South were making great democratic advances. It was during this revolutionary period that Black former slaves and poor white farmers united against the Southern planter to establish the only democratic regime the South has ever known. In areas like South Carolina, Mississippi and Louisiana there was self-government throughout the Black Belt counties and dominant Black representation in the state legislatures. We have already given a detailed narrative of how Black people led the way in making some of the greatest democratic advances of the 19th century and how these advances were squashed in a murderous campaign of sheer terror by the deposed planter class and their capitalist allies in the North.

We have shown how the rise of imperialism, world war and revolution impacted the struggle for Black Liberation and its growing national consciousness. We have looked at the emergence of a Black class-conscious working class rising up in the era of imperialism and linking up to the international struggle against imperialism. So now we must examine the exact nature of the relationship between Black liberation and the international socialist movement spearheaded by the Communist International. And there is no better way of doing that than to look at how the Communist International's position on the Black Liberation movement led to the complete reorganization of the Communist Party in the United States. First let's look at Communist International's position and the line of march they proposed.

The winter of 1928 was a decisive moment in the history of the struggle against imperialism. Preparations were being made for the Sixth Congress of the Communist International. The Anglo-American Secretariat of the Communist International had established a special subcommittee to prepare a draft resolution for the official Negro Commission of the congress. Harry Haywood was one of the five people on this subcommittee (according to Haywood there were four Blacks and one white). There was general agreement that the Communist Party in the United States had grossly underestimated the revolutionary potential of the Black Liberation movement. But there was a basic disagreement as to the source of the Party's underestimation. Most of the members of the subcommittee, including Haywood, took the position that the source was white chauvinism; that it was white chauvinist attitudes and prejudices that led to incorrect policies. The Bolsheviks, approaching it from a Marxist-Leninist perspective, took a different position. In fact, they maintained that the American comrades had stood the whole matter on its head, because the denial of the revolutionary character of the Black Liberation movement came from a fundamentally incorrect social democratic line which rejected the national character of the question. This rejection leads to the false conclusion that only the direct struggle for socialism is revolutionary and that Black people fighting for national liberation somehow distracts from the struggle for socialism and is therefore reactionary. The social democrats deny the National Question and the ultra-left advance the concept of "pure proletarian revolution."

Moreover, one has to be careful so as not to get caught up in the ideological tendencies of racism which sees the struggle as simply a fight against racial prejudices of white people. This approach overlooks the economic and social roots of white chauvinism and denies the defeat of the agrarian democratic revolution initiated during Reconstruction that is still pivotal in the struggle for Black equality in the United States. To be sure, Reconstruction demonstrated that in the South, self-determination for Black people (i.e. Black political power including using force of arms) was the guarantee of Black equality.

But these were not just theoretical discussions. Another Black comrade, James Ford, in his presentation to the Sixth Congress was quick to point out that of the 19 resolutions from the Comintern to the U.S. on party work regarding Black liberation not even one had been put into effect; and he further pointed out that there were only 50 Black people in the party out of a population of 12 million Black Americans.

Thus, the tone was set for the Sixth Congress to carry out with unprecedented determination a radical reevaluation and criticism of the work and policies of the U.S. Communist Party. After much discussion, the party's position—that any type of nationalism among Black people was reactionary—was rejected because that position saw only "pure proletarian" class struggle as the sole revolutionary struggle against capitalism. Nationalism was not a foreign transplant but sprang from the soil of super-exploitation and oppression of Black people in the United States.

The resolution that came out of the Sixth Congress with representatives of revolutionary movements in colonies and semi-colonies around the world rejected the assimilationist theories that previously guided the Communist Party, and defined the Black Liberation movement as "national and revolutionary" in character because the various forms of oppression of Black people, concentrated for the most part in the South, provide the objective and subjective conditions for a national revolutionary movement. Black people in the South were not reserve armies of bourgeois reaction but a revolutionary force to be reckoned with and led by Black workers.

The new party line called upon the party to implement a program calling for complete and real equality, for the elimination of every kind of racial, social and political inequalities. "...its task will be to destroy all together the barrier of race discrimination that has been used to keep apart the black and white workers, and weld them into a solid union of revolutionary force for the overthrow of the common enemy."[13]

The great historic importance of the Sixth Congress of the Communist International is that after a profound discussion and analysis of the question of Black liberation it was resolved that Black people in the United States are an oppressed nation entitled to the right to self-determination—the very thing that Martin R. Delany, the African Methodist Episcopal Church and others were demanding nearly a century earlier. The resolution of the Sixth Congress was founded on the actual, objective, historically evolved situation of Black people in the United States and the theoretical principles first set forth by Lenin and later developed by Stalin. As pointed out above, Lenin had raised the question of Black people as an oppressed nation in the Second Congress of the Communist International. In an accompanying note to his "Theses on the National and Colonial Question," Lenin wrote:

> I would request all comrades, especially those who possess concrete information on any of these complicated problems, to let me have their opinions, amendments, addenda and concrete remarks in the most concise form (no more than two or three pages) particularly on the following points: Austrian experience; Polish-Jewish and Ukranian experience; Alsace-Loraine and Belgium; Ireland; Danish-German, Italo-French and Italo-Slav relations; Balkan experience; Eastern peoples; The struggle against Pan-Islamism; Relations in the Caucasus; The Bashkir and Tatar Republics; Kirghizia; Turkestan, its experience; Negroes in America...[14]

---

13 Foster, *The Negro People*, 455.
14 Lenin, "Draft Theses on National and Colonial Questions for the Second Congress of the Communist International."

The reason for this laundry list of oppressed nations is that Lenin saw the necessity of a concrete analysis of the concrete conditions in each situation of national oppression to avoid an abstract posing of the problem of bourgeois democracy in general and the national/colonial question in particular. The bourgeoisie puts forth the proposition that everyone is equal (under the law) as a weapon against the abolition of classes. Whereas communists maintain that the real meaning of the demand for equality consists in its being a demand for the abolition of classes.

Our fundamental task as Marxist-Leninists is to expose through organized struggle, agitation and propaganda the lies and hypocrisy of bourgeois democracy. As the champions of international proletarian struggle, we must base our policies in the struggle for national liberation of oppressed nations and colonies. Such policies are not based on abstract and formal principles but on a precise and scientific examination of the specific historical situation that brings into bold relief the economic conditions and subsequently making a clear distinction between the interest of the oppressed classes, the ruling classes and the so-called national interest. An equally clear distinction must be made between the oppressed, dependent and subject nations and the oppressing, exploiting and sovereign nations, to expose and counter the bourgeois-democratic lies designed to conceal the colonial and financial enslavement of the vast majority of the world's population by an insignificant European/American minority of the richest and most advanced capitalist countries, a feature characteristic of the era of finance capital and imperialism.

The proletarian and the working masses of all nations must unite in joint revolutionary struggle to overthrow the bourgeoisie and the landlords. It is this unity alone that will guarantee victory over capitalism and imperialism and make a pathway for humanity to abolish national oppression and inequality.

This is how Lenin and the Bolsheviks placed this critical policy question:

> In all their propaganda and agitation—both within parliament and outside it—the Communist parties must consistently expose that constant violation of the equality of nations and of the guaranteed rights of national minorities which is to be seen in all capitalist countries, despite their "democratic" constitutions. It is also necessary, first, constantly to explain that only the Soviet system is capable of ensuring genuine equality of-nations, by uniting first the proletarians and then the whole mass of the working population in the struggle against the bourgeoisie; and, second, that all Communist parties should render direct aid to the

revolutionary movements among the dependent and underprivileged nations (for example, Ireland, the American Negroes, etc.) and in the colonies.

Without the latter condition, which is particularly important, the struggle against the oppression of dependent nations and colonies, as well as recognition of their right to secede, are but a false signboard, as is evidenced by the parties of the Second International.[15]

Marxist-Leninists, having developed the teachings of Marx and Engels in the era of imperialism, addressed the following three questions or problems:

1) What is the basic contradiction driving monopoly capitalism in the era of imperialism?

2) How the immediate question of socialism is brought about by the proletarian (communist)-led revolution seizing power and establishing the dictatorship of the proletariat.

3) The obligation of the Communist International is not to merely issue manifestoes, declarations and proclamations but to give aid and rally the toiling masses of the world in their struggles against imperialist domination and wars.

In 1952 Foster published the *History of the Communist Party* wherein he acknowledges that

> The Communist Party has contributed a number of new and vital features to the struggle of the Negro people: (a) It has elevated this question to its proper high political status, in the realization that the oppressed Negro people are the greatest of all allies of the workers in the class struggle; (b) It has expressed boundless confidence in the feasibility of mass Negro-white co-operation, finding many form and issues for bringing this about; (c) It has raised the theoretical level of the Negro question to that of a National Question, thereby providing the Negro people with their true perspective as an oppressed nation; (d) It has singled out the insidious danger of white chauvinism in the broad working class and in its own ranks has fought against it as no other organization has even began to do; (e) It has considered the Negro question as a key question by which to measure the class integrity and understanding of every individual and organization in the broad labor movement.[16]

---

15   Lenin, "Draft Theses on National and Colonial Questions for the Second Congress of the Communist International."

16   Foster, *History of the Communist Party*, 562.

Two years later, when McCarthyism and repression were running rife, Foster published *The Negro People in American History* wherein he states

> The American Communist Party got its eventual understanding of the Negro question in the United States from the writings and personal counsel of Lenin. This was one of the many basic services to the American labor movement rendered by the Communist International, but it was not realized until 1929...the Socialist Party and the Socialist Labor Party before it had held to the erroneous theory that there was nothing special about the Negro question, that it was simply a part of the general problem of the working class. This led to almost complete passivity regarding the distinct and terrible grievances of the Negro people—lynching, Jim Crow, disfranchisement, and all the rest. At the time the left-wing, which finally developed into the Party, did not clearly challenge this white chauvinist, opportunist position of the Socialist Party and the Socialist Labor Party...This program in theory and practice uniting the struggle of the working class and the Negro people, had to be learned from the Communist International and Lenin.[17]

Also, it is precisely in this book that Foster traces the development of the national consciousness of Black people from the Colored Convention Movement to the Garvey Movement and the African Blood Brotherhood.

In Summary, there are Ten Major Points We Want to Emphasize

Following in the wake of the Russian Revolution, which culminated in the workers seizing power, the consolidation followed by unification of the two communist parties in the United States was complicated by the Palmer Raids and the parties' semi-legal status which took up the whole decade of the 1920s.

In fact, what facilitated the consolidation of the two parties was the Communist International arming the party with the Marxist-Leninist theory of revolution in general and contributing to their theoretical understanding of the question of Black liberation as a National Question. The most vital and difficult part of the transition of the U.S. communist parties into a Communist Party based on Leninist standards was its evolution with respect to this question (which is illustrated by the quotes from Foster above). This ideological flaw which had ossified into dogma had to be corrected for the party to appreciate and fully embrace the revolutionary

---

17   Foster, *The Negro People*, 454.

character of the Black Liberation movement. In other words, the two old communist parties in the United States were infected with the idea of the "pure class approach" rooted in the economist opportunism of the Second International and vulgarized in the expression that the solution of the labor question (which is socialism) would automatically lead to Black liberation. This position not only overlooked the special needs and demands of the Black Liberation movement but bypassed and ignored the immediate struggle against lynching, disfranchisement and social inequality. William Z. Foster honestly states in his *History of The Communist Party* that the Communist Labor Party "did not mention the Negro question at all" because they believed "The racial expression of the Negro question is simply the expression of his economic bondage, each intensifying other..."[18]

The drastic shift in the relationship of forces during the beginnings of the Great Migration and World War I brought about by the rapid rise of the Black industrial proletariat had already set in motion a social movement to unify Black and white workers, as was evidenced by the courageous work of the IWW and Black Wobblies like Ben Fletcher. This movement paved the way for breaking with right-opportunist socialists and "pure proletarian revolution" socialists; it paved the way for breaking with this trivial and cowardly past that gave in to Jim Crow practices instead of taking up head-on the fight against racism and standing in unconditional solidarity with the struggle for Black Liberation. The Communist International, Black revolutionaries and revolutionaries in the colonies and oppressed nations provided the necessary catalysts in the transition for founding new communist parties whose new battle cry would be "Workers, Toilers in the Colonies and Oppressed Nations of the World Unite!"

As a result of the outstanding work of Black communists, their allies in the Communist International and some American white comrades, there developed within the party a campaign for a mass approach that would appreciate the national aspects of the Black Liberation movement. Thus, in the years 1924-25 the party, in alliance with the African Blood Brotherhood, began to reach out to Black people. One of their first recorded acts was participation in the "All-Race Assembly, the Sanhedrin". It was also the first attempt to create a Black united front and it failed. The fact that it failed totally was due in no small measure to the domination of this assembly by the Black petit bourgeoisie (led by the conservative Black intellectual Kelly Miller) and the almost total absence of Black workers, farmers and sharecroppers. The next effort to reach out came in 1925 with the

---

18   Foster, *History of the Communist Party*, 171-172.

establishment of the American Negro Labor Congress (ANLC) whose central objective was to create a viable organization of Black labor to carry on the fight against Black exclusion from organized labor and where necessary to form Black unions. While the Congress attracted very few delegates at their initial meeting, it "...did bring to public attention the full communist program for Black rights"[19] and encouraged the formation of a core of young Black communists. It failed in its mass approach and performed more like a propaganda club for the Communist Party.

In the years referred to above one must remember that the theoretical controversy regarding the National Question as it applied to Black people and conditions unique to the United States was ongoing and by no means settled. Consequently, the style of work of the party proceeded along the line of least resistance, which means that Black comrades led the charge and became the principal agents of party work with Black people. Clearly this was not working, and it became painfully obvious that this work had to be taken up by the whole party and not be compartmentalized in a commission or forum led by Black comrades.

To effectively combat "white chauvinism" and racist attitudes within the party all comrades and not just Black comrades must be engaged in the fight for Black Liberation and at the same time they must vigorously fight against racism in the ranks of the party, the workplace and the community. The deep and abiding mistrust of white people can only be effectively challenged in practice and is exemplified when white communists stand in unconditional solidarity with the immediate demands and long-range goals of the Black Liberation movement.

What is it that makes Marxist-Leninists unique? What makes Marxist-Leninists unique is the very fact that they took up the ideological struggle against the Second International social democrats and the left-opportunist "pure proletarian revolution" approach, based on recognizing the revolutionary nationalist component of the Black Liberation movement. By the same token what makes the American communists unique is that they were a part of the Communist International and were therefore in the best position to receive Lenin's and Stalin's critical contribution to a correct scientific understanding of the National Question in general and the Black liberation question in particular. They were provided by the Communist International with the unique opportunity to see in theory and revolutionary practice how the struggle for Black Liberation links up to the international struggle against imperialism and strategically relates to the struggle for socialism. This singular contribution put the party in the historically

---

19   Allen and Foner, *American Communism*, X.

unique position of being the only predominantly white organization to fight openly against racism in its own ranks while at the same time standing in unconditional solidarity with Black people in their fight for self-determination and national liberation.

What won over the advanced sections of the Black proletariat to the Communist Party was their confidence and trust in the Communist International, which from the very first took an uncompromising stand against national chauvinism and the racist attitudes of the Second International; and in word and deed supported the liberation struggles of all colonial peoples for their independence and their right of self-determination. The super-exploited, nationally oppressed Black people of the United States perceived a friend and invaluable ally in the Communist International.

It was the theoretical insights of V.I. Lenin that laid the scientific basis for understanding the National Question in general and the Black liberation question in particular. After studying the conditions of oppression of Black people in the United States in the era of imperialism with a view toward the composition of the country Lenin wrote:

> They [Black people in the U.S.] should be classed as an oppressed nation for the equality won in the Civil War of 1861-65 and guaranteed by the Constitution of the republic was in many respects increasingly curtailed in the chief Negro areas (the South) in connection with the transition from the progressive, pre-monopoly capitalism of 1860-70 to the reactionary monopoly capitalism (imperialism) of the new era, which in America was especially etched out by the Spanish American imperialist war of 1898.[20]

In their documentary history of the Communist International on the question of Black liberation in the United States the editors Foner and Allen made the following pertinent assessment of Lenin's theoretical contribution:

> ...Lenin saw American Blacks as an 'oppressed nation', a condition arising from their history of oppression within the semi-feudal agrarian system of the South. It was not by mere chance, but the result of years of observation, that in his famous 'Theses on the National and Colonial Questions,' submitted to the IInd Congress, he urged that 'all Communist parties should render direct aid to the dependent and

---

20   Lenin, quoted in Foner and Allen, *American Communism*, xiii.

underprivileged nations (for example, Ireland, American Negroes, etc.) and in the colonies.'

One can well surmise that Lenin singled our Ireland and the American Negroes for mention from scores of eligible examples because he was aware of the chauvinism of the English toward the Irish and of the Americans toward the Negroes. In fact he had made note of the chauvinism of the American white workers regarding the Chinese and Japanese exclusion acts, as well as the racism of the American Socialist Party regarding them and the American Negroes.[21]

A Passing Note on Black-White Working-Class Solidarity

While there can be no question of the great theoretical contribution Lenin and the Communist International made to our understanding of the Black liberation and the National Question in the United States, still we must take note of how Black and white workers had to deal with persistent problems of disunity fueled by racism in the face of intensified exploitation and the necessities of class struggle.

Looking at our history from the perspective of class struggle we see that there have been historic moments of Black-white working-class solidarity throughout history, going all the way back to colonial times and coming through slavery, Civil War, Reconstruction and the early dawn of imperialism. And in every period, in every stage of the struggle for Black Liberation there exists this question of unity and the struggle for Black and white unity. But it must be recognized that no group has fought for this unity more courageously and consistently than Black workers themselves.

Under the most wretched conditions of colonial oppression, slavery, war and post-Civil War counterrevolution, the rise of monopoly capitalism and the social savagery of Jim Crow, Black workers fought their way into organized labor to become some of the most militant and class-conscious organizers in the labor movement.

We have outlined in previous chapters how the internationalist socialist movement (led by Marx and Engels) that emerged in 1848 recognized that labor in a Black and white skin must be united, and that this unity was essential to the development of a class-conscious working class pursuing the revolutionary path to socialism. The communists, when first arriving on the American scene after 1848, at once united with Black workers and

---

21   Lenin, quoted in Foner and Allen, *American Communism*, xiii.

the abolitionist movement. They fought for Black and white unity in the trade union movement and for the abolition of slavery.

With the rise of the Second International we saw how the revolutionary essence of Marxism was betrayed by the reformist-revisionists and national chauvinists. It was Lenin who restored the revolutionary essence of Marxism as we entered the new era of imperialism. But in the very year of triumph of the Russian Revolution (1917-18) one of the greatest concrete steps made in the fight for unity was made in Chicago, the hub of the industrial working class in America. It happened in the wake of the ending of World War I when Black workers and the most class-conscious white workers united in the campaign to strike the meatpacking industry in Chicago.

The communist party of a new type was yet to be born but William Z. Foster and J.W. Johnstone, who would be pioneers in creating a new Marxist-Leninist party, were in the thick of the struggle to create Black-white unity in the packing house strike movement during this period. Out of a total of 200,000 packing house workers nationwide, with Foster and Johnstone being the catalysts, 20,000 Black workers were successfully organized into the union. This was an unprecedented achievement surpassing the I.W.W, the Miners, Longshoremen and all unions friendly to the cause of Black workers. It set the tone for the role of communists in the oncoming class battles in the era of the Great Depression. It is well worth quoting Foster's summary of this historic breakthrough:

> The newly-developed solidarity of Negro and white workers in the packing industry had a real test of fire during the severe Chicago "race riots" of July 1919. This anti-Negro pogrom was organized by agents of the packers, who above all wanted to force the Negroes out of the unions and to drive a wedge between the Negro and white workers in their plants. The Chicago Stockyards Labor Council, then headed by J.W. Johnstone...saw the storm coming and mobilized the union membership to head it off. On July 6th a big parade of white and Negro packinghouse workers marched through the Negro districts of the South Side of Chicago, in an effort to allay the grave tension. Nevertheless, on July 27th, as a result of direct provocation by packer-organized hoodlums, the storm burst. Virtual civil war raged for two weeks in the whole area, with 6,000 police and soldiers mobilized to intimidate the Negro people. Meanwhile, 30,000 white stockyards union members met, protested, pledged solidarity with their Negro brother workers, and demanded the withdrawal of the armed forces, which had done most of the killing. The splendid stand of the Stockyards Labor Council during this crisis, and especially of Jack Johnstone, stands forth as one of the very finest events

in the history of the labor movement. It did much to cement Negro-white labor solidarity over the country.[22]

This is just an historical demonstration of the scientific truth that objective social relations determine our social consciousness and the fact that the strategic importance of Black-white working-class solidarity is rooted in the fight against racism and national oppression. This historically determined reality asserts itself on the battlefields of class struggle with iron necessity, independent of communists in the United States consciously recognizing, grasping and developing a theoretical understanding of Black liberation as a National Question. After the Sixth Congress this fact would be clearly demonstrated as a matter of policy, of theory becoming a material force through practical implementation.

---

22   Foster, *History of the Communist Party*, 231.

8

Black Liberation and Class Struggle During the Great Depression, the Rise of Fascism and World War II

World War I was more than just the senseless slaughter of 10 million on the battlefields of Europe and 20 million dying from hunger and disease precipitated by the war. The roots of the war can be found in the colonies. They had been maintained and regulated by a ruthless regime of terror going back to the commercial warfare of slavery and the colonial carnage unleashed on humanity during that unparalleled era of conquest and plunder, done under the pretense of spreading European civilization in the name of Christianity. It was a war between the colonial powers over boundaries and territories, of re-dividing an already conquered world by the ancient principle of might makes right. The monopoly capitalist countries of Europe were competing for spheres of influence; for Alsace-Loraine, the Balkans, Africa, the Middle East, India and China. World War I was claimed by U.S. President Woodrow Wilson as a war to end all wars; it was claimed by the national chauvinists of Europe as a war that would seal the destiny of Western civilization and remove all doubt about the master race residing in Europe.

With these hypocritical lofty aims concealing the horrors of colonialism, imperialism tolls the bells for the old "progressive" order of ascending capitalism, and also ushers in the new imperial order of decaying monopoly capitalism. The working class in the advanced capitalist countries, driven by the objective conditions created by intensified capitalist exploitation, rebels and advances toward social revolution, but due to the treachery and national chauvinism of the Second International is not conscious enough or organized enough as a class for itself to overthrow capitalism. The revolt of the proletariat in the advanced capitalist countries was defeated. But not in Russia, the most backward country of Europe, the weakest link in the imperialist chain. In Russia, the proletarian-led revolution was victorious and it immediately (as a matter of revolutionary principle and in the face of counter-revolution) formed alliances with the anti-colonial, anti-imperialist struggles of the East, Africa and the world.

With the end of the war came the beginning of revolution. With the end of the war there rose up in the East a section of humanity who had been enslaved in factories, herded in congested slums and trampled underfoot by landlords. This Russian revolution had earth-shaking power because it united with those in the colonies whose lands were stolen, whose human essence was denied while their culture and way of life was being murdered for the sake of construction of roads and railroads, canals and runways for the colonialist to make off with the plunder. The days of prosperity and relative stability that rested on the pedestal of colonial slavery and the semi-feudal, backward capitalist countries of Europe was over, for imperialism, in unleashing a war also ushered in an era of social revolution.

There is no question that the outbreak of World War I was both a reflection and expression of the world crisis of capitalism—of monopoly capitalism choking the organization of production and exchange, and the drive of imperialism in the face of dwindling markets to further divide and re-divide the world and to open new markets to intensify the looting of the colonies and the exploitation of the workers.

Here is how Lenin summarized the tasks of communists in what he characterized as a European war:

> First, all-embracing propaganda, involving the army and the theatre of hostilities as well, for the socialist revolution and the need to use weapons, not against their brothers, the wage slaves in other countries, but against the reactionary and bourgeois governments and parties of all countries; the urgent necessity of organizing illegal nuclei and groups in the armies of all nations, to conduct such propaganda in all languages; a merciless struggle against the chauvinism and "patriotism" of the philistines and bourgeoisie of all countries without exception. In the struggle against the leaders of the present International, who have betrayed socialism, it is imperative to appeal to the revolutionary consciousness of the working masses, who bear the entire burden of the war and are in most cases hostile to opportunism and chauvinism.
>
> Secondly, as an immediate slogan, propaganda for republics in (Germany, Poland, Russia, and other countries, and for the transforming of all the separate states of Europe into a republican United States of Europe.
>
> Thirdly and particularly, a struggle against the tsarist monarchy and Great-Russian, Pan-Slavist chauvinism, and advocacy of a revolution in Russia, as well as of the liberation of and self-determination for nationalities oppressed by Russia, coupled with the immediate slogans of a

democratic republic, the confiscation of the landed estates, and an eight-hour working day.[1]

Humankind had entered a new era of capitalism, the era of imperialism where the periodic cyclical crises of capitalism typical of the previous era is replaced by a general crisis. This general crisis opened in 1914 and erupted into the new violent explosions of world war.

What distinguishes the general crisis is that it represents capitalism in its decline as opposed to its rise. The inherent contradiction of socialized production vs. private appropriation still exists but it takes on new forms and an intensified character. During the old cyclical crises of overproduction there were always, as Marx pointed out, "momentary and forcible solutions of the existing contradictions, violent eruptions, which restored the disturbed equilibrium for a while." Readjustment involved such drastic measures as destroying massive food surpluses to permit the resumption of production on a higher plane; knocking out the smaller, inefficient or less efficient business owners; destroying some capital in order to save some capital and in order to affect a further concentration of capital. These measures generally led to the resumption of production at a higher level. However, with the general crisis of 1914 the domination of the world by the imperialists is complete. By the beginning of the 20th century there is no more world to be divided up. Under imperialism, capitalism has come to a dead end. The era of expansion had developed into the era of contraction, and the principal political reason for this was that the Soviet Union had taken one-sixth of earth's land mass from imperialism and consequently became a center for world revolution.

The era of imperialism, infected with the crises that come with decay, is also the era of socialist revolution and national liberation. The general crisis of capitalism admits of no solution—unemployment and poverty are seen for what they are, necessary and permanent features of capitalism.

Nonetheless, when the war ends, the imperialists, despite the "menace" of socialism and national liberation, still attempted to inaugurate a period of restoration with the declared aim of restoring capitalism to at least its pre-war normalcy. It did not get recognized on all sides that old conditions had passed beyond resurrection—until the stock market crashed in 1929.

There is an important prelude to the rise of fascism in Europe after World War I and in the wake of the revolutionary wave of workers'

---

1   Lenin, "The Tasks of Revolutionary Social-Democracy in the European War," in *Collected Works*, accessed on December 4, 2020, https://www.marxists.org/archive/lenin/works/1914/aug/x01.htm.

rebellions that sweep across Europe at that time. That prelude was American exceptionalism, the Roaring Twenties, when it seemed as if capitalism's resilience was bringing in its wake an era of stability and prosperity. The popular song was *Happy Days Are Here Again!*

F. Scott Fitzgerald's jazz era, the so-called "golden age" of prosperity, hedonism and excessive flouting of wealth, power and prestige saw its end come abruptly. Men accustomed to lighting their Cuban cigars with $100 bills suddenly found themselves penniless and jumping from tall buildings.

The crisis was one of overproduction, driven by the greed for profit and the competitive social savagery of capitalism that puts profit before people. Marxist-Leninists saw it coming, because they did not buy into the reformist drivel about American capitalism being unique and exempt from the laws of growth and decay; they saw the crisis coming and were developing a plan to fight back, from a revolutionary perspective, at the Sixth Congress of the Communist International.

The reformist drivel we speak of was being peddled by a faction in the party led by Jay Lovestone and other petit bourgeois intellectuals. They were counter-organizing and pushing the line that industrialization of the South would liquidate the question of Black liberation. This position was arrived at as a result of the development of a whole body of revisionist theory in the party by professional factionalists. These opportunists argued that American capitalism, unlike European capitalism, was stable and enjoyed an era of prosperity akin to the Victorian Age of British capitalism. Carrying this inverted analysis out to its logical conclusion, one might say American capitalism, being stable and in a progressive swing of industrial growth, faces no impending crisis, and with the growth of Black industrial workers in the South the question of nationhood or special demands is obsolete.

Still, as pointed out above, the Great Depression came as predicted by Marxist-Leninists who carried the day at the Sixth Congress. And communists committed to carrying out the line of the Sixth Congress were gearing up for the fight.

William Z. Foster sums up the Marxist-Leninist perspective on the oncoming crisis, said he:

> The outbreak of the economic crisis did not take Marxists of the world by surprise. They had understood from the outset of the Coolidge boom period that the capitalist "prosperity was built upon sand." Repeatedly during these years the Marxists, notably in the speeches of Stalin, had pointed to the coming of an economic crisis in the United States. The American Communist Party had analyzed indications of the

approaching crisis, namely, the prolonged agricultural depression, the big unemployment in coal mining, textiles, and other industries, and the deadly overproduction effects of the speed-up and low wage policies of the bosses and their agents, the top trade union leaders. At its meeting in February 1928, the Central Committee of the Communist Party warned that serious cracks were appearing in the American economy and that these would grow and have far-reaching effects…during the fight against Lovestone in 1927-29, a key matter of dispute was precisely the economic prospects of the United States. Lovestone contended that whereas other parts of the world might become involved in economic crisis, the United States, in an exceptional position, would continue indefinitely upon an upward spiral of development; whereas Marxists in the Party maintained that a great American economic crisis was in the making.[2]

The Great Depression shook the very foundations of imperialism in America and around the world and communists were called upon to meet the challenge to unite the workers, the peasant toilers and oppressed nations of the world to fight back not only for what had been lost but for a new world a coming, for national liberation and socialism.

In 1927 the great, pioneering Black sociologist E. Franklin Frazier made the observation that "There are two types of businesses in New York in terms of Negro hiring policies: those that employ Negroes in menial positions and those that employ no Negroes." Being super-exploited by the monopoly-capitalist and used like a hammer for depressing wages, Black workers, and especially Black women workers, were already in an acute state of economic depression. The average weekly pay of Black working women was about $6 a week.

With the serious decline in cotton production in 1923, farm workers were pouring into the cities looking for jobs. Technological changes were also pushing Black landless peasants into the cities looking for jobs. The growth of Black workers in industry had come to a halt.

Black workers were experiencing depression-levels of unemployment. By the early months of 1929, while the economic goose of prosperity was still flying high, 300,000 Black industrial workers were thrown out of work, i.e., one-fifth of Black industrial workers. Impoverished white workers were replacing Black workers as waiters, hotel workers, door men, bellhops and elevator operators. In the South, ditchdiggers turned white.

---

2   Foster, *History of the Communist Party*, 277-278.

Theory Meets Practice in the Dirt and Blood of Battle

Harry Haywood was returning home. He had been one of the delegates to the Sixth Congress of the Communist International and had been in the Soviet Union studying Marxism-Leninism and participating in the ideological struggle regarding the question of Black liberation. Upon arrival in the U.S., Haywood went straight to Harlem.

Here was the legendary Black metropolis; here in the 1920s is where the revolutionary fire of Black Liberation was rejuvenated and nurtured; here is where Haywood returned, armed with the science of Marxism-Leninism, holding steady in the courage of his convictions and prepared to test his ideas in the dirt and blood of battle.

As soon as he set foot in East Harlem, he witnessed what the first year of the Great Depression had done. He saw the stark reality of poverty and the expression of hopelessness on the faces of the people. But beneath that hopelessness and glaring despair was seething restlessness, rage and the agitated existence born of poverty and oppression.

The Great Depression signaled the worst of times, where the poor would have to pay for the crimes of capitalist greed, yet communists saw it as the best of times in which to launch the League of Struggle for Negro Rights (LSNR). This new organization would replace the American Negro Labor Council, which had come under sharp criticism for its inadequacies and sectarianism. In the letter and spirit of the resolution on the question of Black liberation coming out of the Sixth Congress, the LSNR was prepared for battle.

The LSNR would be the vehicle for forming a united front movement around the party's program for Black liberation. However, Haywood did not step into a situation that had been impatiently waiting for him; social movements, driven by objective social relations, wait for no one.

On the eve of the Great Depression, desperate, rebellious coal miners defied the leadership of the national United Mine Workers, and with the leadership of the Communist Party, went on strike in the coal fields of Ohio and Pennsylvania. Every strikebreaking tactic imaginable was used. Families were evicted from company houses, strikers were curbed by court injunctions, gun thugs and company cops and state police raided miners' barracks and strikers' tents, and worst of all, Black and white scabs were imported.

Then on September 28, 1928 there occurred an event indicative of a turning point in history. Six-hundred coal miners met in East Pittsburgh, Pennsylvania to form the National Miners Union (NMU). Mobs armed with clubs and knives attempted to disrupt the miners' convention. There was violence in the streets and around the hotel. As things finally got underway the meeting convened and William Boyce, a Black miner, was elected vice president. He not only opposed strikebreaking but was able to win Black miners to the NMU. Boyce's message was a simple one; he reminded Black miners of how the United Mine Workers banned discrimination in their constitution while practicing it at the same time. John Lewis, president of the United Mine Workers, had been presiding over Jim Crow practices, whereas the NMU was fighting it and Black miners were leaders of this union which stood and fought for economic, political and social equality.

That is how the struggle for unity between Black and white workers erupted with NMU communist leadership. And yet another challenge came in 1929 when a strike broke out in the southern Illinois coal region and the communists continued to push and fight for unity. However, they were able to win only a short-lived, fragile unity that fell apart.

On new battlefields in the Pittsburgh area again, where in 1930 Isaiah Hawkins, a veteran of the Negro Miners Relief Committee emerges as the full-time head of the union's Negro Department.

Now in 1931 the NMU is leading a major strike in Pittsburg and West Virginia. According to Phillip Foner, 42,000 miners walked out; 6000 were Black. In the Pricedale mines of Pennsylvania's bituminous region, Black workers refused to join the strike. The NMU threw a picnic and had Black communist organizer Richard B. More to come in and address the Black miners and their families. More, in a fiery speech, united with NMU's stand against Jim Crow practices, praised the Black and white unity of the workers, linking their struggles to the economic crisis, rising unemployment, the Scottsboro case and the long and bitter struggle for Black liberation and working-class solidarity. The next day Black miners at Pricedale joined the strike.

The Great Depression was on and the strike dragged on. Meanwhile the NMU had initiated organizing drives in the Kentucky counties of Harlan and Bell. Black and white miners united were involved in pitched, bloody battles in Harlan County. Militant Black workers Essley Phillips and Goines Eubanks were indicted on framed-up murder charges.

Only 300 to 400 Black workers joined the strike, but this communist-led union insisted on equality. William Boyce, a Black militant miner from Indiana and the national vice president of NMU, stated it clearly, said he:

> But the National Miners Union wants the Negro miners… To build the NMU means building a bulwark of defense to Negro miners…in the

NMU the Negro is not a dues paying member, silent, bulldozed, discriminated, but an active leading part of the directing councils of the organization itself.

Every Negro should join the National Miners Union because it fights vigorously for full economic, political and social equality for them. It fights discrimination, segregation, Jim-Crowism and disfranchisement. In the NMU the Negro miners have a valiant defender.[3]

Unity wasn't a given in the face of desperation. Unity had to be fought for no matter what. For example, some strikers argued that the kitchen area should be segregated because they didn't want to give the mine operators an excuse to raid them on the pretext that local Jim Crow ordinances were being violated. Communists stood their ground and argued that Black and white workers must stand together in unshakable unity. In defiance of Jim Crow, the workers ate in the same kitchen area.

The fact that communists fought against Jim Crow practices is of paramount importance. Uncompromisingly opposing Jim Crow in the shops and raising the issue of the special oppression of Black workers became one of the identifying characteristics of communists working in the Deep South and the nation.

In organizing the needle trades industry in the early 1930s, communists, led by Maude White, took on the challenge of handling the complaints of Black women workers. Addressing the subcontracting of the labor of Black women by white pressers was a priority. White disapproved of how communists in the shops avoided confronting this issue because of fear of "antagonizing the white pressers." White was informed by her comrades that the union handled all complaints "in the same manner." It was then that White raised the hard questions such as: Don't Black people suffer from special oppression? In fact, doesn't the boss treat Black women and white women differently? If the union is not taking a stand against this blatant discrimination, then the union is "capitulating before the white chauvinism of the boss."

White not only led the fight against "capitulating to white chauvinism," she demonstrated that communists must fight for unity by showing how discriminating wage differentials created by sub-contracting hurts all workers. This is how communists led the struggle in the trade union movement. No matter the obstacles or difficulties, Maude White and her party held fast to the notion that communists, as a matter of principle, must press for action on the special needs and demands of Black workers.

---

3   Foner, *Organized Labor*, 195.

Organizing the Working Class in the Deep South and the National Question

If the South is the physical, geographic location of the Black nation then it stands to reason that this is where revolutionaries need to focus their time energy and resources. Let us focus on at least two areas in the South where the class struggle and the struggle for Black Liberation merged and reached a level of intensity not seen before or since.

I — North Carolina

In the 1920s the textile industry in North Carolina was booming like never before. New mills were springing up all over the place. Investors from the North were pouring money into this area because of its abundant supply of cheap, non-union labor. It was boldly claimed by advertising and marketing agencies that operatives of Southern mills were so intelligent and enterprising because workers worked longer hours for less pay, raised their own food and needed less clothing than their counterparts up North. Thus, this was the ideal situation and moment for the capitalist bosses to apply the newly found principles of scientific management by reducing the labor force and ensuring that each worker was more "efficient," that is, did more work in the same time with no raise in pay, or even a reduction in pay.

The National Textile Workers Union saw this as one of those instances in which intensification of exploitation created opportunities to organize the workers into the union. Depression was looming on the horizon, labor conditions were worsening, unemployment was high and workers were ready to fight.

The fight began at the Loray Mill in Gastonia, North Carolina. It was the largest mill in the state and was owned by a textile company in Rhode Island. Many workers responded to the union drive, joining the union. The company retaliated by firing those who joined. There was a strike vote and 1800 workers refused to return to the mill and demanded:

— Elimination of all piece work, hank or cloth systems, and substitution of a standard wage scale.
— A minimum standard weekly wage of $20.
— Forty-hour, five-day week.
— Abolition of all speeding and doubling up of work.

Figure 11 — The Loray Mill in Gastonia, N.C.

— Equal pay for equal work for women and youth.
— Decent and sanitary working and housing conditions.
— Immediate installation of baths without extra charge to workers.
— Screening of all homes without extra charge to workers.
— Repair of toilets in mill.
— Reduction by 50 per cent of rent and light charges.
— Recognition of the union.

The owners rejected the workers' demands and refused to negotiate. Some workers returned to work; others remained on the picket line even after being evicted from their company owned homes. They were forced to live in a tent village established by the union. Hostilities erupted when deputies and company goons attacked the picket line, which was composed mostly of women and children.

Fred Beal, union organizer for National Textile Workers Union and Carl Reeve of International Labor Defense issued the following statement:

> Those who are fighting the battles of the mill owners organized a lawless mob and wrecked our headquarters, then arrested the strikers who were there defending it and charged them first with 'damaging property' and 'disorderly conduct.'
>
> The deputies and soldiers, if they did not actually participate, stood and looked on without interfering. A pair of handcuffs was found in the

ruins, as well as bullet shells such as are used by the deputies and guardsmen. The tools used by the mob were tools which had on them the Manville Jenckes label and are used within the mills. This frame up is as obvious as the fake bomb plot perpetrated a few days ago.

The acts of this lawless mob prove to the population that our opponents will use their hired thugs and gangsters and go to any length to try to prevent relief and try to starve the strikers out. The authorities cooperated by arresting and in at least one case brutally beating unarmed strikers. The workers of the town are greatly indignant and the strike has been materially strengthened by this outrage. We are establishing new headquarters and as a result of the outrage hundreds of new members are flocking into our union from the Gastonia mills.

There is no split in our union. Our ranks are as strong as ever. There is no division. Proof of this is the splendid spirit of the strikers and the huge mass meetings held. We will carry out our program of organizing the thousands of textile workers in this section—spreading the strike. The strike at the Manville Jenckes mill is in a healthy condition. We will win.[4]

Beal was attacked for being a "red" and being paid by a communist organization. Somehow that was supposed to make the demands of the workers invalid. The workers closed their ranks and continued to fight back.

Hostilities erupted again when on,

...June 7, 1929, deputies and company gun thugs broke up a picket line composed largely of women and children. The deputies and other police officers then went to the tent village, shots were fired, and the Gastonia police chief, Orville F. Aderholt, was killed.

Sixteen union members were tried for the murder of Aderholt and were released when a mistrial was declared in September 1929. The troubles in Gastonia continued. At a large rally of union workers on September 14, 1929, Ella May Wiggins, a popular speaker known for her ballads in support of working women, was killed. Wiggins' death helped bring attention and sympathy to the plight of the mill workers, but it was not enough to secure a victory for the unions. Although workers received some relief from federal and state legislation in the 1930s, employers were successful in keeping unions out of the state, a legacy that has continued to the present. As of 2003, only 3.1 percent of North Carolina's

---

4   "Beal Blames Mill Forces For Recent Strike Outrage," *The Gastonia Daily Gazette*, April 20, 1929.

workers were members of unions, the lowest representation in the United States.[5]

Now in the Southern textile mills about 5% of the workers were Black, working at the bottom of the occupational structure as handlers and porters. In Gastonia they labored in a miserable waste mill that was attached to the Loray mill. "The NTWU," writes Mark Solomon, "initially had trouble recruiting them, but as a result of pressure from the Party, the Gastonia local launched an organizing drive among blacks that netted seventeen members."[6]

The strike in Gastonia was the catalyst in creating a union organizing drive throughout the South on the eve of the Great Depression. As we have already stated above, communists saw the Great Depression coming and were gearing up for a fight; well, that fight began earnestly in Gastonia. It represented in that moment the conscious awakening of the working class and it assumes the position of uniting with the fight for Black liberation. It represented the first uprising of any significance after the overthrow of Black Radical Reconstruction, which had been a decade-long battle for democracy betrayed by the emerging industrial monopoly capitalists of the North. In part, Reconstruction represented an uprising of landless Black peasants just freed from chattel slavery and poor white farmers, while Gastonia represented the opening salvo in a class struggle against the capitalist bosses (the new wage-slave masters of the South) united with the Black struggle against Jim Crow and for self-determination.

The party had not yet fully and consciously adopted the policy of the Sixth Congress addressing the question of Black liberation, but here they were in the belly of the beast pursuing the line of march before the line was formally adopted, practicing their way into correct thinking.

II — Alabama

Now let us move on to Birmingham, Alabama, the industrial capital of the South, where the working-class movement and the struggle for Black Liberation merge into one of the most powerful movements of the 1930s and

---

5   Nicholas Graham, "June 1929: Strike at Loray Mill," *NC Miscellany*, June 1, 2004, https://blogs.lib.unc.edu/ncm/2004/06/01/this_month_june_1929/.

6   Solomon, *The Cry Was Unity*, 109.

that set the tone for militant struggles against Jim Crow and created the foundation for the Civil Rights movements of the 1950s and 1960s.

Birmingham is a unique Southern city set in a ten-county region at the root of the Appalachian mountain chain. This is perhaps the richest mineral region of the South in coal and iron ore. Birmingham is in Jefferson County, which is undisputedly the wealthiest county in ore deposits and mines producing annually about half of the coal in Alabama. The entire state during the good years produced over 20 million tons of coal (i.e. 3.5 to 4% of the total amount of coal mined in the United States). From its share of the iron ore, nearly 3 million tons of pig iron was produced. In 1929 there was 1,216,334 gross tons of rolled steel products. Two-thirds of the steel output was concentrated in the Birmingham area which includes the industrial towns of Bessemer, Ensley, Wylam and the enclave of Fairfield. According to the 1930 census Birmingham's population was 250,000 with about 100,000 being Black. The gainfully employed were counted at 173,031 and 96,295 were white and 76,736 were Black. In other words, 55% of the total was white workers and 45% was Black workers.

Looking at figures for the laboring force of Alabama in iron and steel 13,331 of 19,392 were Black workers, i.e., 68.74%. For the City of Birmingham Black workers were 5,364 of 7,222 or 74.27%.

The rocket-like rise of this new industrial center in the heart of Dixie carried the New South promise of cheap, non-union labor as the basis of prosperity. But millions of workers and sharecropping farmers caught in the economic noose of the oncoming Great Depression were beginning to doubt this New South lie of Jim Crow capitalism. As one writer put it: "In good times white workers could feel superior to African Americans who dug ditches, stripped tobacco leaves in factories, or swept up cotton lint; all that was 'nigger work.' In bad times whites wanted those jobs."[7] It is into this situation that communists went and raised the red banners of class struggle and Black liberation. Alabama, for some of the objectively stated reasons given herein above, was the point of concentration. But let us quickly add that those who carried the principal burdens of the struggle, those who most frequently died in the dirt and blood of battle were not outside agitators, they were the native daughters and sons of the South. And it has been noted, even by bourgeois historians who peddle the anti-communist message of the ruling class, that Black and white workers and Black and white landless peasants united and fought back courageously

---

7   Glenda Elizabeth Gilmore, *Defying Dixie: The Radical Roots of Civil Rights*, 1919-1950 (W. W. Norton, 2009), 108.

under the most dire and life-threatening circumstances. Now let us take a deeper look at some of these battles and see who rose to the occasion.

The most important thing about the Communist Party taking up the struggles in the deep South is the fact that it knew it was consciously intervening in an ongoing class struggle and a national liberation struggle that was driven by the social and economic misery created by the Great Depression. It knew that it was entering the fray now based on a theoretical understanding of the question of Black liberation that called for a strategic alliance between the working-class warriors fighting for socialism and Black freedom fighters struggling against national oppression.

Given the social reality of Jim Crow segregation, the white communists dispatched into the South had no organized roots among white workers. The party had to overcome the hurdles of rejection and legalized repression and terror while at the same time grappling with the fact that "the movement attracted overwhelming numbers of Black working people."[8] This situation resulted in the formation of a broad-based organization of Black folk and a small cadre of white Northern comrades and with a few local supporters who had to operate underground. It was clear that the party in the South had to become, in the words of William Z. Foster, the party of Black people to have a future. And so, it did.

In the spring of 1932, Black communists Hosea Hudson, Joe Howard and Andy Brown, coming straight out of the Birmingham proletariat, led a march of some 125 to 150 Black relief workers who were being forced to do back-breaking road work in exchange for a small pittance for relief. It was a three-mile march through hostile territory. By the time the marchers got to the city hall steps there were about 50 people left. Joe Burton, a Black Young Communist League leader, was knocked down by police officers. The police drew guns and trained them on the crowd while Burton, bleeding, rose to his feet, declaring that the people will return in greater numbers.[9]

The communist-led demonstrators returned to the Jefferson County courthouse November 7, 1932 5,000 to 7,000 strong. There were arrests, a white Birmingham-born communist and Alice Burke were among those arrested. Mary Leonard led the delegation that met with Jimmie Jones to present the demands of the local Unemployed Councils demanding food and cash relief. Their demands were denied, and the police forced the

---

8   Robin D. G. Kelley, *Hammer and Hoe: Alabama Communists During the Great Depression* (University of North Carolina Press, 1990), 30.

9   Hosea Hudson and Ralph David Abernathy, *Black Worker in the Deep South: A Personal Record* (International Publishers, 1972), 55-57.

crowd to disperse. But these protests of the unemployed, involving several thousand Black and white workers, continued for months and were part of a national campaign of the National Committee of Unemployed Councils and the National Hunger Marchers.

Although these mass demonstrations mainly pushed economic demands for jobs, food and public relief, they also coincided with and were linked to the party's election campaign. For the very first time in history the Communist Party could register and officially place their candidates on the ballot in Jefferson County, Alabama. At the top of the national ticket was William Z. Foster for president and James Ford (a leading Black communist) for vice president. In Birmingham, the two local communist candidates were Lee Parson, a Black worker from the Ninth Congressional District, and Andrew Forsman, a white pioneer organizer for the Knights of Labor and short-term president of the Mobile Trades Council, who was running for the U.S. Senate. James Ford, being from Alabama and a former steelworker provided great inspiration and encouragement.

Birmingham communists hosted a campaign meeting to be attended by Foster. The response of the City Commissioner Jimmie Jones was that if Foster made any "remarks that are in violation of the law" he would be arrested. The meeting was scheduled for the night of October 9 and since Foster had taken ill, Clarence Hathaway, editor of the *Daily Worker* was to speak in his place. Hathaway, however, ended up being detained by the police in New Orleans and so he too was unable to make the meeting. Yet the meeting went on as planned and about 1,200 people showed up at a popular theater in the Black community. There were speeches about the election campaign, the unemployed movement, and the campaign to free the Scottsboro boys. The meeting was disrupted when Klansmen in the audience ignited a smoke bomb.

Despite fierce opposition from the white power structure with their KKK terrorists, the Ford-Foster ticket polled 726 votes from disfranchised Black folk and poor white farmers. Jefferson County's Black majority districts polled 33 votes for Foster-Ford and 133 for Lee Parson. This is quite remarkable considering the blatant and officially sanctioned terror tactics used against Black people trying to vote. The Sharecroppers Union was active in northern Alabama and developing a following among poor white farmers. This is where most of the 726 votes came from.

The next battle came on May Day, May 1, 1933, when the workers rallied to protest the municipal government's failure to provide adequate relief for the unemployed. Twenty thousand Black people, 27% of Birmingham's Black population, were on relief rolls. The city had revoked the march permit of the demonstrators, but this did not stop the demonstration. Three thousand people showed up at Ingram Park and were met by police, Legionnaires and Klansmen. Jane Speed, a white worker standing in the midst of a crowd of Black women jumped up on the bumper of a car and shouted, "Fellow workers, is this the way they do." She was immediately arrested. There ensued a shoving match which quickly escalated into the violence of a street brawl. An officer shoves a gun into the side of a Black woman and she yells, "Shoot me and you shoot a thousand more."

The unemployed campaign brought into the party 5,000 dues-paying members. The party's campaign to help the jobless was part and parcel of the campaign to organize the unorganized into the union and Alabama, the industrial center of the South, was the ideal place. The tactics of confrontation and resistance developed on the battle fields of Birmingham not only led to the development of cadre (especially among Black women) but also prepared the party for its future work in the mines, mills and the Black Belt plantations.

These struggles, with Black-white unity at their base, were historic and earth-shaking in that nothing like this level of political activity and economic struggle had happened since Black Reconstruction.

The struggles we have outlined are more than just moments of history in which the class struggle and Black Liberation movement merge into one unified revolutionary movement creating a tidal wave for social change. They are also more than a historical demonstration of the objective and subjective basis for Black and white unity. These struggles show that, driven by the realities of class exploitation and national oppression, the Communist Party became actively engaged in confronting Jim-Crowism in the South in particular and the country in general. Fighting Jim Crow and advancing the national question and the class struggle at the same time was the invaluable contribution communists made to the Black Liberation movement.

The party started saying to white workers (even before it had settled accounts on the Black liberation question) that you cannot advance or improve your situation as long as you allow the capitalist bosses to divide you from your fellow workers based on race discrimination that condemns them to the worst jobs and the lowest pay. But more than this, organized labor must stand in solidarity with Black people in their struggles for the most elementary bourgeois democratic rights to vote and to overturn the tyrannical system of institutionalized racism that subjects them to lynching and other forms of mass violence and state sanctioned violence that took their lives and destroyed their properties.

These advances took place while the Communist Party was still caught up in the snares of its past error of not recognizing the impact of racism on the party itself. This inherent blindness can only be overcome when the party becomes armed with the scientific approach developed by Lenin and Stalin on the national question and its application to the question of Black liberation. This correct, Marxist-Leninist formulation of the question of Black liberation put the party in position to go forward with testing these ideas in the struggle and developing them as a result of concrete analysis of concrete conditions.

As we have outlined above, the party fought side by side with Black workers and farmers, united with white workers and farmers, in the cotton fields, coal mines, textile mills, steel mills, packing houses and warehouses and loading docks and shipping docks. The Communist Party's application of the Marxist-Leninist program formulated at the Sixth Congress of the Communist International in 1928 strengthened and gave rise to the mass participation of Black workers, farmers and sharecroppers in the struggle against Jim Crow and the class struggles in the South and throughout the country. All the while they conducted a relentless and uncompromising struggle for Black and white unity, and against national oppression, racism and repression.

The Great Depression, Budding Fascism and the Second World War

The South, being the most backward section of the country, of course led in fascist tactics and ideology when confronted with a rising, militant proletariat that was fighting its way into class consciousness based on solidarity with the Black Liberation movement. The rebellion of the workers and Black people in the South were confronted by KKK-led mobs and fascist Black Shirts. The Black Shirts were a paramilitary fascist group modeled after Mussolini's Black Shirts; their stated goal was "saving jobs for working class white men."

The Black Shirts offered starving white workers an easy solution to unemployment: the extension of segregation. Taking white supremacy to its next logical step, it advocated the relocation of African Americans to rural areas, thus reserving urban wage labor for whites. Scarce jobs and miserly municipal relief would be reserved for whites, while agriculture would flourish with an ample supply of cheap Black labor. The white working-class men who joined the Black Shirts abhorred the paternalistic relationship between comfortable white men and their Black servants, and they resented the monopoly that Black men had on certain service jobs.

> "You men who freely tip your caddies, your bootblack, your waiter, and everyone else who serves you," the *Black Shirt* asked, "do you realize the fact that there are several thousand unemployed white men..." "In a quandary on how to replace your [Black] servants? The Black Shirt can furnish you any kind of white help," the organization boasted.[10]

The Loray Mill lawyer, Major Alfred Lee Bulwinkle, who defended the murderer of the striking textile worker Ella May Wiggins, ran for Congress in 1930 with the backing of the Black Shirts, the Charlotte Central Labor Council and the state American Federation of Labor. This unholy alliance backed by the mill owners sent Bulwinkle to Congress. This is how a fascist movement was budding in the South, a region seasoned with acts of terrorism against Black people and steeped in the doctrine of white supremacy.

The spirit of rebellion and budding fascism in the 1930s, the period of the Great Depression, was not confined to the South. The poverty created by joblessness and dispossession was widespread and popularized by John Steinbeck in his novel *The Grapes of Wrath;* there were masses of people hungry, homeless and destitute in every sense of the word. There was great social unrest and the imminent danger of social rebellion morphing into social revolution. Here's a litany of events and news that attest to the diversity of this social uprising:

— January 3, 1931: About 500 mostly white farmers, some of them armed, march on the central business district of England, Arkansas demanding food for themselves and their families. They threatened to take foods from the stores if their demands were not met.

— July 9, 1931 in Detroit, Michigan: 500 unemployed men rioted after being turned out of a city lodging house for lack of funds. This uprising was violently repressed by the police.

— August 5, 1931: 1,500 jobless men in Indiana Harbor in East Chicago, Indiana stormed the plant of the Fruit Growers Express Company demanding jobs to keep from starving. The company's response was to call the police who in turn brutally attacked the jobless with clubs.

---

10   Gilmore, *Defying Dixie*, 110.

— April 1, 1932, Chicago: 500 school children march on the Board of Education demanding food.

— Boston June 3, 1932: Two dozen children raided a buffet set up for the Spanish War vets. Two squads of police drove them away.

— January 21, 1933: Several hundred jobless folk surrounded a restaurant just off of Union Square in New York City.[11]

These news-reported events could be multiplied by the thousands just for the period 1931-1933.

This objective state of affairs reflected in these reports was clearly indicative of the fact that the post-World War I attempts to restore capitalist stability had only limited success with piecemeal reforms, and had failed utterly by 1929 and the opening decade of the 1930s.

We have already offered a brief analysis as to why this happened but in the interest of continuity some points need to be restated. We have seen that with World War I coming to a close, there was an onrush of workers' rebellions in some of the most industrialized European countries like Germany. These rebellions were drowned in blood and this was made all the more possible by the unholy alliance of social democracy with capitalism. The sole strategic aim of this alliance was to defeat the socialist revolution and if this meant some immediate concessions to the workers, then so be it. This alliance was held together by the conviction that capitalism had embarked upon an age of prosperity that could be equally enjoyed by the capitalist bosses and the workers.

The great communist theoretician R. Palme Dutt writes,

> Only by hiding capitalism under a Social Democratic front was the capitalist state saved after the war. Social Democracy united with capitalism to defeat the workers' revolution. A great show of concessions to the workers was made; promises were lavishly broadcast; Socialization Commissions, Nationalization Commissions, Sankey Commissions were set up; wages were increased and hours shortened.[12]

Indeed, there were concessions and promises to no end. And based on what appeared to be unparalleled advances in production, trade and profits, both the ruling class and social democrats believed that they were standing on the threshold of a period of unending prosperity. "The outlook

---

11   Zinn, "Self-help in Hard Times," *A People's History of the United States*, 277-298.

12   Palme Dutt, *Fascism and Social Revolution: A Study of the Economics and Politics of the Extreme Stages of Capitalism in Decay* (International Publishers, 1935), 49-50.

of the world today," said President Hoover one year before the stock market crash, "is for the greatest era of commercial expansion in history."

The year before Hoover's declaration, Dutt wrote a book entitled *Socialism and the Living Wage*, exposing the clay feet of the American Colossus, the Ford vs. Marx myth, and the class collaboration policies of the social democrats. The British labor press reviews rejected Dutt's analysis on the grounds that Marx's theories only applied to 19th-century capitalism and were outdated and refuted by the new era of modern capitalism demonstrated by the American miracle. The United States had become the Holy Land of capitalism, with the industrial monopoly capitalist Henry Ford as its prophet.

Social democrats could hide but not erase the contradictions of capitalism. In Europe, even during the era of prosperity when capitalist stability was successfully restored, the temporary gains of the workers were quickly reversed by a capitalist backlash, as it were, pushing workers' wages back to pre-war levels. The social democrats were relegated to the role of the "loyal opposition," and once again the workers were disillusioned and fed up with the reformist strategy and tactics of the social democrats. Thus, in Europe, capitalism proceeded to seek a new basis and we saw the rise of the national socialist movements (i.e. fascism) as a complement to the already existing national chauvinism of social democracy. Dutt wrote,

> The third weapon of capitalism in the re-establishment of its power and its economic system was the drawing on the colossal reserves of the still unshaken center of world capitalism—American capitalism. American loans and credits poured into Europe to bolster up and rebuild the shaken fabric of European capitalism. On this basis the restoration of the gold standard took place. The triumph of stabilization was celebrated by the bankers of the world. It was obvious that this basis was a false one, and would involve a boomerang outcome, as was predicted at the time by Marxists.[13]

But as we have seen, this great American structure of capitalism which had provided the economic base for rebuilding world capitalism came crashing down in 1929 and so ended the era of illusions propagated by the capitalist bosses and the system of closed financial oligarchies that used the state to maintain the predatory practices of monopoly capital, that is the practicing of super-exploitation of the toilers in the colonies and intensified exploitation of the international proletariat. It was becoming clear to workers

---

13   Dutt, *Fascism and Social Revolution*, 50.

that capitalism/imperialism as a working system was no longer working. Now to maintain itself, capitalism had to pass the burden of the Depression on to the working masses. Dutt again:

> When the crash came with the world economic crisis, the conditions of monopoly capitalism still further prevented the "normal" working out, and intensified and prolonged the crisis. The great capitalist monopolies were able to maintain relatively high profits in the midst of the depression, by artificial measures of restriction, by maintaining monopoly prices above the general price-level, and by passing on the burden of the depression to the working masses, to the petit bourgeoisie and to the colonial peoples. The prices of cartelized goods in Germany in the beginning of 1933 had only fallen 20 per cent below the level of the first half of 1929, whereas the price of non-cartelized goods had fallen 55 per cent...The prices of manufactured goods in the imperialist countries were maintained above the pre-war level, at the same time as the price of the raw-material products of the colonial peoples were depressed to an average of half the pre-war level. But this meant to intensify the contradictions at the root of the crisis. In this way the workings of monopoly capitalism hindered the "normal" solution of the crisis after the methods of "healthy" capitalism.[14]

The intensification of "the contradictions at the root of the crisis" also reflected itself in the thinking of the ruling class monopoly capitalists in that they were forced by the circumstances of the collapse of the world market to admit that the failed attempts to "restore" capitalism in the 1920s were based on myths and illusions and had no foundation. The 1929 stock market crash condemned to the dustbins of history the principal illusion that in the post-war decade there had emerged a "super capitalism" that could perpetually improve the standard of living of the working masses without class struggle and that some form of "ultra-imperialism" was bringing a new world order of peace and prosperity. As Dutt points out, it was precisely the collapse of this illusion that led the development of capitalist ideology to fascism. No longer dazzled by the rapid recovery of capitalism in the post-war period, the monopoly capitalists were now prepared to opt for open terroristic dictatorship. And this would be the final solution to workers' rebellions in the industrial nations and uprisings in the colonies (i.e. struggles for national liberation).

Fascism was the ruling class's answer to mass rebellion of the workers. The workers and the farmers were demanding immediate relief from

---

14   Dutt, *Fascism and Social Revolution*, 51-52.

hunger and unemployment and a new social and economic order empowering the people to enjoy the prosperity they create. A conscious struggle for socialism led by communists in America and throughout the world was clearly an essential part of the workers' rebellion and the blossoming struggles for national liberation in the colonies and Black liberation in the United States.

Fascism as Counter-revolution

Fascism arose in Europe in the 1930s and unleashed on humankind one of the most massive carnages in the history of the world. It was not merely a populist movement arising out of the very real suffering of the masses during a worldwide depression. No. In terms of its class nature it was as Dimitrov described it:

> Comrades, the accession to power of fascism must not be conceived of in so simplified and smooth a form, as though some committee or other of finance capital decided on a certain date to set up a fascist dictatorship. In reality, fascism usually comes to power in the course of a mutual, and at times severe, struggle against the old bourgeois parties, or a definite section of these parties, in the course of a struggle even within the fascist camp itself—a struggle which at times leads to armed clashes, as we have witnessed in the case of Germany, Austria and other countries. All this, however, does not make less important the fact that, before the establishment of a fascist dictatorship, bourgeois governments usually pass through a number of preliminary stages and adopt a number of reactionary measures which directly facilitate the accession to power of fascism. Whoever does not fight the reactionary measures of the bourgeoisie and the growth of fascism at these preparatory stages is not in a position to prevent the victory of fascism, but, on the contrary, facilitates that victory.[15]

The source of the reactionary measures of the bourgeoisie is the revolt of the masses against the wretched economic and social conditions precipitated by the increasing polarization of wealth and poverty under capitalism. This as a general proposition can be demonstrated in every phase of capitalist development when the class struggle heats up and the ruling class responds to political rebellion with political repression. The class-struggle

---

15 Georgi Dimitrov, *The United Front: The Struggle Against Fascism and War* (Intentional Publishers, 1938), 12.

dynamics that gave rise to fascism have the same general character pinpointed by Dimitrov, but to concretely make the connection of how the reactionary measures of the bourgeoisie contributes to the growth of fascism, let us quickly review what happened in Italy and Germany.

The revolutionary wave precipitated by World War I swept not only over Russia but most of Europe. The formation of the Communist International was crucial to the consolidation of the victory of the Bolsheviks. But also, it was crucial to the revolutionary success of the proletariat and the peasants in those countries where objectively the masses were already in revolt.

In Italy, for example, there was a large-scale strike movement and the peasants were seizing land. The Italian Socialist Party, having gotten rid of a significant portion of their class collaborationists and inveterate social reformers, grew from 24,000 members in 1910 to 70,000 by the end of the war in 1918. In 1919, they affiliated with the Communist International and went to the elections on a communist platform calling for the dictatorship of the proletariat. They won 156 out of 508 seats making them the strongest party. The fascists under the leadership of Mussolini did not win a single seat. Party membership quickly rose to 200,000. Then came the municipal elections of 1920, when the party won control of over 2,000 cities and towns. The workers were seizing and occupying factories. The government no longer had the ability to rule in the old way and revolution seemed imminent.

Expectations for social revolution were high and yet the actions of the party did not measure up; it refused to give revolutionary leadership in this impending class war. In October 1920, the Communist International complained:

> The P.S.I (Italian Socialist Party) acts with too much hesitation. It is not the Party which leads the masses, but the masses which push the Party...In Italy there exist all the necessary conditions for a victorious revolution except for one—a good working-class organization.[16]

At the precise moment the Communist International set forth the above stated complaint there was no communist party. As Dutt so correctly points out there were anarchists and confused syndicalists on one side and hesitating centralists and vacillating social democrats on the other.

The Italian Socialist Party (PSI) affiliated to the Communist International in 1919 but they retained at the core of their leadership the old

---

16 Dutt, *Fascism and Social Revolution*, 114-115.

reformist leaders who clearly wanted to undermine the communist program and its revolutionary line. Due to this treachery, the watchword of the Italian Socialist Party became: "The revolution is not made. The revolution comes." Consequently, the revolutionaries in the PSI came too late to the realization that the spontaneous uprising of the masses, with all its great sacrifices and boldness, will spend itself out in a multitude of uncoordinated actions in the absence of a revolutionary party. Upon applying for readmission to the Communist International, the PSI leader, Giacinto Menotti Serrati, on behalf of the revolutionary faction declared at the congress: "Our fault is that we never sufficiently prepared ourselves for the events that have overtaken us…Today we believe it essential to abandon the democratic illusion, and to create a combative, active and audacious Party." This was simply post-mortem analysis. Within a month Mussolini was in power; such was the price of defeat for the working-class insurrection in Italy. How so?

In Italy, the way the bourgeois ruling class addressed the workers' rebellion was to collaborate with the socialist reformers to make sure the strike movement and the occupation of factories remained a passive economic movement and not be extended to the conquest of political power, while at the same time supporting the fascist terrorist actions of Mussolini and his political thugs.

How and Why German Fascism Came to Power

Let's start with the Treaty of Versailles. Many bourgeois historians contend that this 1919 treaty, ending World War I, was very harsh and a major factor in the rise of fascism in Germany. But terms of surrender in a war are usually harsh and this is particularly true when you have a clash of empires over a re-division of the world.

When Russia dropped out of the war, Germany and Austria imposed on her the Brest-Litovsk Treaty. Of this treaty, historian Spencer Tucker says, "The German General Staff had formulated extraordinarily harsh terms that shocked even the German negotiator."

When Germans claimed that the Treaty of Versailles was too harsh the Allies held that it was not as hard as the Brest-Litovsk Treaty of 1918 imposed on revolutionary Russia.

The conditions of surrender imposed by the victors were harsh indeed. Germany considered the demand for reparations extremely harsh, being that the country had already been bankrupted by the war. The limit on the size of German armed forces was simply another consequence of surrender. However, the most grievous condition was that Germany was forced to give up her overseas colonies and allow the Rhineland to be occupied and held as collateral for reparations. For this the German imperialists wanted revenge.

While capitalism in 1920s America was experiencing an economic boom, in Germany the masses were impoverished, and the bourgeoisie, having suffered military defeat in the war, was caught in the noose of shame and humiliation and hell bent on punishing the workers for having defied their rule. The country was in a mess, it not only felt defeated but looked defeated in the face of hyperinflation and destroyed savings of millions and widespread destitution. There was near civil war, with rioting in the streets and the perpetual clashing of political parties of the right and left. The government had collapsed, the proletarian revolution was defeated and the Weimar Republic, feeble and unstable, rose out of the ashes.

But how was the proletarian revolution defeated? One could say that fascism in Germany was conceived (i.e. entered its gestation period) when the proletarian revolution was murdered in the cradle in 1918. With the outbreak of World War in 1914 the social democrats had already allied themselves with the Kaiser, leading German workers into the slaughterhouse of an imperialist war, caving into national chauvinism and betraying the revolutionary essence of Marxism. Yet the workers did rise up in 1918, overthrowing the old German state. Dutt writes,

> The Workers' and Soldiers' Councils were supreme throughout the country. The bourgeoisie and old militarist were unable to offer any resistance. All the conditions were present for building an impregnable Soviet Republic—save that no revolutionary party existed to lead the workers (the Communist Party of Germany was only formed in December 1918). The completeness of the proletarian power at the beginning of the revolution, before Social Democracy had squandered and destroyed it, is attested by the principal social democratic witnesses themselves: The military collapse brought the whole power of the state into the hands of the proletarian in one stroke. (H. Ströbel, *The German Revolution*, p. 1)
>
> In November 1918, the Revolution was the work of the proletariat alone. The proletariat won so all-powerful a position that the bourgeois elements at first did not dare to attempt any resistance. (Kautsky, Introduction to the Third Edition of *The Proletarian Revolution*, 1931.)[17]

---

17   Dutt, *Fascism and Social Revolution*, 128.

In the absence of a revolutionary party the proletariat could not move forward and establish the dictatorship of the proletariat. So, what happened in Italy was repeated in Germany and for the same reason; the social democrats were opposed to the revolution. But German fascism still had its own unique course of development for it was Germany that was the most advanced industrialized nation in Europe, with the most class-conscious industrial proletariat in the world. How then does it transition from this to the most monstrous and brutal fascist country in the world? In general, of course, it has to do with revolution and counter-revolution, but what were the concrete objective and subjective conditions that gave rise to the fascists seizing power in Germany?

We've already addressed both sides of the question in noting that even though there was objectively a revolutionary situation in Germany there was no revolutionary party to lead the workers out of their frustration and into seizing power and establishing the dictatorship of the proletariat. Consequently, the uprising of the German proletariat was defeated but the objective conditions that fueled the uprising worsened.

It was not the harsh terms of the Versailles Treaty with its reparations and loss of colonies that brought the fascists to power. It was, as R. Palme Dutt so brilliantly demonstrates in his classic work *Fascism and Social Revolution*, the betrayal of the proletarian revolution by the social democrats. This betrayal provided fuel for the emerging "National Socialist German Workers Party." Now the ruling class would blame the defeat of Germany in WWI on the "Jews and communists, who did the work of the Bolsheviks from within."

The treacherous alliance of social democrats with the conservative, bourgeois chauvinists constituted the foundation of the Weimar Republic, and it was precisely this "Republic" that provided cover for the racist, anticommunist "German Workers Party" led by Anton Drexler.

In 1919 Adolph Hitler, an ex-corporal, was asked by the army to spy on the German Workers Party. In spying on them Hitler discovered that Drexler's views on Jews and world communism were the same as his. He then renounced his job and joined Drexler; together they went on to found the "National Socialist German Workers Party" or the "Nazis." Claiming the Germans to be the "master race" the Nazis proceeded to dump the Treaty of Versailles and took to the streets killing Jews and communists.

Hitler was arrested and there was a mockery of a trial for treason, where he was allowed (by friendly nationalist judges) to make speeches from the witness stand. While in jail he wrote *Mein Kampf* (My Struggle) calling for a return to the golden age of Germany which would be achieved by taking political power from the wimps of the Weimar Republic, getting revenge on the Allied powers and delivering death to the Jews and communists.

The steady deterioration of the economic and social conditions heightened by the 1929 stock market crash meant success for the Nazis; their party would come to have a presence in every major city, exploiting the fears and insecurities of the German people and promising to restore law and order and national pride. The conservatives and the monopoly capitalists forced the weak and senile war hero President Field Marshall von Hindenburg to appoint Hitler chancellor on January 30, 1933. Nazi Germany was born, and social democracy allied with monopoly capital was the midwife.

Fascism and American Exceptionalism

Shortly after Hitler was appointed chancellor, Franklin D. Roosevelt was inaugurated president of the United States. Roosevelt came to power by an election (manipulated and controlled by the monopoly-capitalists) and Hitler came to power by executive fiat (manipulated and controlled by monopoly-capitalists). They were both granted emergency powers (as in war time) to deal with the impending economic crisis and growing working-class rebellion. On inauguration day President Roosevelt declared:

> I shall ask Congress for the one remaining instrument to meet the crisis—broad executive power to wage war on the emergency as great as the power that would be given to me if we were in fact invaded by a foreign foe.[18]

Roosevelt used this "broad executive power" to fashion the New Deal legislation known as the National Industrial Recovery Act. R. Palme Dutt sums up the character of the National Industrial Recovery Act (NIRA), said he:

> The "New Deal," the policy of the Roosevelt regime expressed in the National Industrial Recovery Act and associated measures, represents the most comprehensive and ruthless attempt of finance-capital to consolidate its power with the entire strength of the State machine over the

---

18   Samuel I. Rosenman, ed., *Public Papers and Addresses of Franklin D. Roosevelt*, vol. 2, *The Year of Crisis, 1933* (Random House, 1938), 11-16.

whole field of industry, to hold the workers in subjection under extreme and intensified exploitation with a universal lowering of standards, to conduct on this basis and on the basis of the depreciated dollar a campaign for markets, and to prepare directly the consequent inevitable war.[19]

The primary political objective of the Roosevelt regime was to remove the last vestiges of the anti-trust laws that were hampering the rapid development of the trustification of the basic industries, and other tendencies of high finance banditry. The preamble to the National Industrial Recovery Act clearly states its aim "to remove obstructions to the free flow of interstate commerce which tend to diminish the amount thereof, and to promote the organization of industry for the purpose of co-operative action among trade groups." It's all about guaranteeing profits through regulation of conditions of labor, price-fixing and restrictions on production. This was no different from the political objectives of fascism in Italy and Germany, particularly the war character of the whole system of state organization based on mobilization of industry and conscription of labor. This is what was beneath all the liberal bombast and fake claims of progressive reforms: naked state-sponsored capitalism designed to create industrial servitude of the workers and impoverished peonage for the farmers and toilers. The United States was not exceptional, for like Italy and Germany it too was pursuing a fascist solution. The fascist ideologues and their parties were vying for power here the same as they were in Germany but under different circumstances, conditions and relationship of forces. The most striking historically-determined difference is that World War I was not fought on American soil and so the U.S. was spared the economic, social and cultural devastation of war. What was different from America in Europe was that there was an eminent revolutionary situation in both Italy and Germany.

The reason why we didn't get the open terroristic dictatorship of the bourgeoisie was in part the militant fightback of working people and the nationally oppressed. We have already noted how the conscious intervention of the Communist Party turned spontaneous uprisings into a united organized force of the workers in alliance with the Black Liberation movement. William Z. Foster offers an excellent summary of why the U.S. monopoly-capitalist bosses didn't opt for fascism, said Foster:

---

19   Dutt, *Fascism and Social Revolution*, 267.

(a) U.S. capitalism was not as deeply affected by the general crisis of the system as was German capitalism; (b) U.S. capitalism did not face an eminent proletarian revolution as did German capitalism.; (c) U.S. capitalism belonged during that period to the group of imperialist powers that temporarily favored the maintenance of the status quo in the world relation of forces in the imperialist camp and it was not actively preparing for a world war to re-divide the world as was German capitalism; (d) U.S. capitalism unlike that of Germany, still possessed the financial means to carry out a reform program such as the New Deal, instead of turning to the fateful weapon of fascism.[20]

In broad strokes, this assessment of why no fascist regime came to power here is essentially correct, yet it does not deny the inherent fascist tendencies in the New Deal reform program. As we have pointed out above the monopoly/capitalist bosses were shamelessly using the New Deal to camouflage their industrial control by extending company unionism and subordinating organized labor to the dictates of capital. The so-called "socialists" and the American Federation of Labor leaders united with fascist demagogues like Father Coughlin and Huey Long in support of the New Deal's program of no strikes and other class-collaborationist policies. They joined together in the creation of a fake "national front" supporting the National Industrial Recovery Act (NIRA). The Blue Eagle symbol of NIRA quickly became the symbol of a new right-wing-driven patriotism that denounced opponents of Roosevelt's package as traitors. Everybody was whipped into line except the communists and the oppressed Black masses, other oppressed nationalities, workers and poor farmers. As we have seen, it was precisely the Communist Party, and its willingness to lead what clearly became the biggest mass movement of workers, where the cry was unity, in U.S. history. Despite the Roosevelt regime's call for no strikes there emerged a strike movement. The 1934 national textile strike, led by the United Textile Workers involved 475,000 workers in 11 states, including white and Black workers in the South. As we have already noted above these strikes were met with brutal repression.

By 1936 the unemployed still numbered about 13 million. Upon a proposal from the Communist Party, the Unemployed Councils and the Workers Alliance (founded by the Socialist Party of America) united into one organization. This new level of organization among the unemployed became a powerful instrument of solidarity, making the recruitment of scabs, for the first time in U.S. history, difficult during an economic crisis.

---

20   Foster, *History of the Communist Party*, 296.

Strikes and the massive marches of the unemployed did result in some concessions in the early first rounds of New Deal legislation. The U.S. Supreme Court declared New Deal programs unconstitutional and President Roosevelt moved slightly but decisively to the "left of center," presenting Congress with a second round of legislation creating the Works Progress Administration (WPA), the Wagner Act creating the National Labor Relations Board, and the Social Security Act establishing a safety net of meager federal benefits for the aged, children and the unemployed. Unemployment was down 3 million, profits were significantly up from 1932, and with these national improvements in the economy, the class struggle seemingly cooled down and there were fewer marches in the streets. But at the same time these improvements hardly affected Black people, for they were still hit by an unemployment rate of 50%.

In every part of the country, Black worker unemployment was not significantly reduced by New Deal reforms. The capitalist bosses were still ruthlessly pursuing the racist policy of last hired, first fired. In Black Harlem, 350,000 people lived in congested conditions of 233 persons per acre; this and rapidly deteriorating social conditions led to a violent uprising on the very day that the New Deal reforms were being passed.

In Chicago, the second largest Black metropolis in the U.S., where there was not a lull in the struggle for Black Liberation, the class struggle was starting to heat up again and war was looming on the horizon.

A Note on Mussolini Invading Ethiopia and Chicago Reds

In February 1935, Italian troops were in Eritrea building up for an invasion of Ethiopia. In July 1935 the Communist International opened its historic Seventh Congress in Moscow. These two events not only were powerful signals that the jackals of war were about to be unleashed upon the world, but also the announcement of a historical turning point in the struggle for socialism and national liberation. Among the critical first shots initiating the global outbreak of World War II were those fired in Ethiopia, years before Poland or Pearl Harbor.

The forces of Black Liberation and the Communist Party in Chicago seized the time and proceeded to call for and build a broad united front against Mussolini invading Ethiopia. The Black community, united with communists, held an emergency Southside conference on July 10, 1935, 15 days before the Seventh Congress of the Communist International was convened.

More than 1,100 delegates turned out, representing Black lodges, social clubs, churches, various Black nationalist formations, the YWCA and a number of Italian anti-fascist groups. Harry Haywood, one of the Black communist organizers, said, "Revolutionary-led organizations, such as the ILD [International Labor Defense], the Unemployed Councils, and the League Against War and Fascism, as well as the communist and Socialist Parties, took part. It was a genuine citywide people's front with the Southside as its base."[21]

From this conference the Joint Committee for the Defense of Ethiopia was formed. The Reverend Harold M. Kinsley of the Church of the Good Shepherd was elected chairman of the joint committee, and Arthur Falls, a young Black surgeon, was elected secretary. An action program to mobilize thousands on the Southside for a Hands Off Ethiopia Parade and petition drive for 500,000 signatures was initiated; delegations were quickly formed to visit and reach out to churches and community-based organizations. Delegations were being formed to meet with Mayor Edward Kelly (an open Mussolini supporter) and demand a march permit. The pro-fascist Mayor Kelly refused to give a permit to march. The united front continued to broaden and deepen with endorsements from the Chicago branch of the Socialist Party and the local executive council of the Chicago American Federation of Labor (AFL).

The protest at the Italian consulate was very well-organized and brilliantly executed. Harry Haywood, a known Black communist leader, was in the delegation that met with the consul demanding an immediate withdrawal of Italian troops from Ethiopia and Africa. The slogans "Down with Mussolini!" and "Hands off Ethiopia!" were shouted by protesters in the streets during the meeting with the consulate. Two young women protesters, one Black and one white, were handcuffed to a lamppost while wearing white T-shirts reading "Hands off Ethiopia."

Again, there was a meeting with Mayor Kelly and again a permit for the parade was denied. The organizers proceeded to have a final meeting to prepare for the protest parade. It was decided that the people would exercise their democratic right to march, in defiance of the mayor and police.

Harry Haywood, one of the lead organizers, describes the day of the march as bright and warm with hundreds of cops waiting to bust up the parade. There was a line of paddy wagons near the East 47th Street El Station. Some of the organizers were also waiting but they were hiding on the rooftops ready to spring into action.

---

21 Haywood, *Black Bolshevik*, 448.

Haywood wrote,

> Then the demonstrators began arriving; streams of them, striding expectantly down the steps from the El station. And the action began. The police assumed most whites getting off the El in this part of town, the heart of Black Chicago, must be there for the demonstration. They began indiscriminately herding them into patrol wagons and hustling them off to the station. They limited the arrests among Blacks to a few well-known leaders. The whole police plan was orchestrated by Mike Mills of the Chicago Red Squad. Their strategy was to spare Blacks the brunt of the attack because a direct attack in this part of town could set off a full-scale riot. In this way they hoped to split the demonstrators and thus make it easier to disperse them.
>
> From my vantage point [on the roof-top], I could see the scene unfolding. Pandemonium broke loose—the streets were crowded with demonstrators and shoppers alike. As arrests were made, people began shouting protests and slogans. I saw Oliver Law jump up and begin addressing the crowd from a roof very near the El station.
>
> This caught the police off guard, and it took some time before they could get to him. But as soon as Law was pulled down and arrested, another speaker began on the roof across the street. This was repeated five or six times as the police moved frantically to silence the speakers. By this time the crowd had grown considerably and the street and sidewalks were jammed. Every time we would outsmart the police, a great roar would go up from the crowd, and every time another arrest was made, they would jeer the cops. Milton Howard, the *Daily Worker's* man-on-the-spot, described the scene:
>
> "There were 2,000 uniformed police with revolvers and clubs lined up through a quarter mile radius from the corners where the demonstration was to have begun.
>
> "But the 10,000 Negro and white enemies of war gathered to raise their voices in solidarity with the independent Negro country facing the war menace of fascist troops were not easily intimidated. Driven and herded from one corner to another, dispersed by proddings from clubs and revolver butts, scattered groups held stubbornly the immediate neighborhood from the early afternoon far into the night so that hundreds of police had to set a ring of isolation around the area several blocks on either side, blocking all traffic in their fear of a demonstration. Despite provocations, the assembled thousands permitted no breach of their peaceful discipline. The only violence was the slugging of helpless prisoners by the police and detectives in police cars and vans. For many blocks on either side of Prairie and Forty-Seventh Streets police cars guided by members of the 'Red Squad' cruised everywhere, stopping and searching cars, seizing every white person in sight, chasing 'suspicious'

> Negroes and whites down alleys, swinging clubs and blackjacks in an or-
> ganized sweep of brutality under the 'Red Squad' leader Lieutenant Mike
> Mills."[22]

It was a tug of war, with police pushing, antagonizing the crowd and arresting people. Haywood spoke to the crowd from a rooftop, pointing out
that Mayor Kelly and Police Chief Allman had brought the fascist street
brawling tactics of Mussolini to Chicago. A *Chicago Defender* reporter who
witnessed the bloody scene reported:

> If the people who saw the police break up the parade were surprised at
> the brutality that went on all afternoon on 47th Street they would have
> been astonished at the downright savageness with which the police
> amused themselves at the Wabash Avenue Station. The Patrol wagons
> gathered in such numbers in front of the station to hold up traffic on
> 48th Street. Prisoners were unloaded in the middle of the thoroughfare.
> On each side of the wagon formed a long double line of 15-30 police.
> The unfortunate prisoners were pulled out of the vehicle and forced to
> run the gauntlet. Their heads, shins and bodies were clubbed by police-
> men who yelped in glee at the bloody sight.[23]

On the streets of Chicago's Black community, in the dirt and blood of
battle, a united front against fascist aggression and fascism was being
forged. This was prior to the Seventh Congress of the Communist International being convened and Dimitrov giving his historic presentation
calling for a United Front against fascism. History waits for no one and
objective social relations are always prior to subjective evaluation. Consequently, Marxist-Leninists are always raising the banner of truth from the
battlefield of awesome deeds, bearing witness to the fact that we continu-
ally practice our way into correct thinking.

Summing Up the International
Situation Going into World War II

It was the October Revolution of 1917 that gave birth to the concept of a
proletariat-led worker-peasant alliance. The proletariat (especially in developing countries) must accomplish the socialist revolution by allying to
itself the semi-proletarian masses and peasants to crush the resistance of

---

22 Haywood, *Black Bolshevik,* 453-455.
23 Haywood, *Black Bolshevik,* 455.

the imperialist-backed national bourgeoisie by revolutionary means (i.e. force) in order to bring to a halt the instability of the peasantry and the petty bourgeoisie. This principle is an abiding one and that it is embodied in the class war cry: "Workers and Oppressed Peoples of the World Unite, You have Nothing To Lose But Your Chains and a World to Gain!"

The Bolshevik Revolution was the first to show us how, practically and theoretically, to carry out the democratic revolution to completion and move on to the building of socialism. The Bolshevik Revolution was the first to show us the need for a communist party, a revolutionary vanguard, an advanced detachment, to help carry out the democratic revolution and lead the people in the building of socialism. This fundamental advance in Marxist theory and practice was brought about by Lenin—it represented a change in attitude toward the peasantry and colonized toilers, it inaugurated a policy of including the peasantry in the ranks of the revolutionary forces that the working class could lead.

Stalin, in the *Foundations of Leninism*, defines Leninism as Marxism in the era of imperialism. He also saw the Bolshevik Revolution as a turning point in history, marking the imperialist era as also the era of socialist revolution. Before Lenin, Marxism was confined to Europe; with the advent of the October Revolution, under Lenin's and the Communist Party's leadership, the doctrine of Marxism became relevant to the entire world, and especially to the colonized world of oppressed toilers.

Hence, socialism was no longer just a question for the industrially advanced countries of Europe. The Russian communists, by theoretically postulating and carrying out in practice this proposition, demonstrated that the transition through stages to socialism is the course that all countries in the world, no matter their degree of capitalist development, must follow in the struggle for socialism and the liberation of humanity from capitalist bondage.

Lenin has taught us that in the age of imperialism, capitalism arrived at its final stage, where periodic wars for re-dividing an already divided world is a necessary consequence of uneven development, reflecting the relative strengths of the different imperialist powers. Under imperialism all humanity is engulfed in the general crisis of decaying capitalism and periodic wars.

Before the Great Depression of 1929, Stalin identified these three principal contradictions of decaying capitalism in the era of imperialism:

1) The contradiction between labor and capital, 2) the contradiction between the various imperialist powers in the struggle for sources for raw

material and foreign territory and 3) the struggles between a handful of so-called "civilized" nations and the millions of colonially oppressed peoples.

In 1930, during the worldwide depression, Stalin not only added the existence and thriving of socialism (for socialism was experiencing phenomenal growth in this period) and decaying capitalism as a contradiction, he said that by its very existence the Soviet Union was revolutionizing the international working class. The growth and political might of the Soviet Union vs. the international crisis of capitalism was the driving force of the contradiction between imperialism and socialism. This contradiction had primary importance because the working people of oppressed, colonized nations are subjected to the most brutal forms of capitalist exploitation and are used as cannon fodder in imperialist wars of aggression. Because in the era of imperialism, capitalism has become historically obsolescent, it is the harbinger of world revolution. The Bolshevik Revolution ushered in a revolutionary era where socialism became an imminent phenomenon, a matter of practical choice for those nations fighting against colonial oppression and living under the scourge of imperialism.

Here's how Lenin put it: "If on the one hand the economic position of the masses has become intolerable, and on the other hand, the disintegration described by Keynes has set in and is growing among the negligible minority of all-powerful victor countries, then we are in the presence of the maturing of the two conditions for the world revolution."

The Bolshevik Revolution and its contribution to the world revolutionary process came during World War I, that is, prior to the rise of fascism, World War II and the era of decolonization. It came at precisely the right time. To paraphrase Stalin, it came at a time when the social savagery of imperialism had made socialism a practical choice for all humanity.

Two conclusions derive from this understanding. 1) That all countries had to proceed through various routes to socialism as a pre-condition to their liberation from capitalist enslavement; and 2) because imperialism linked all countries together in a chain, their liberation was interconnected. The Russian Revolution broke the chain of imperialism at its "weakest link," thus setting off a chain reaction that would lead to the collapse of imperialism. Out of this arises the Communist International (Third International) inscribing on their banners the following revolutionary call:

> Colonial slaves of Africa and Asia! The hour of proletarian dictatorship in Europe will strike for you as the hour of your own emancipation!
>
> The entire bourgeois world accuses the communists of destroying freedom and political democracy. These are lies. Upon assuming power, the proletariat merely lays bare the complete impossibility of employing

the methods of bourgeois democracy and creates the conditions and forms of a new and much higher workers' democracy. The whole course of capitalist development, especially during its final imperialist epoch, has acted to undermine political democracy not only by dividing nations into two irreconcilably hostile classes, but also by condemning numerous petty-bourgeois and proletarian layers, as well as the most disinherited lowest strata of the proletariat, to economic debilitation and political impotence.

In those countries where historical development provided the opportunity, the working class has utilized the regime of political democracy in order to organize against capitalism. The same thing will likewise take place in the future in those countries where conditions for the proletarian revolution have not yet matured. But broad intermediate masses not only in the villages but also in the cities are being held back by capitalism, lagging entire epochs behind historical development.[24]

With the coming of World War II, the Communist International came to a close and socialism in the land of its birth was fighting for survival. But world war did not succeed in wiping out socialism. In fact, socialism gained new ground and national liberation movements sprung up in Africa and Asia like mushrooms after the rains.

Clearly the fascists were defeated in War World II by an alliance of the Soviet Union, Great Britain, France and the United States. The united struggles of the peoples of China, so-called Indo-China, Indonesia, the Philippines and the South Pacific prevailed against Japanese imperialism. How this alliance against the fascist hounds of war in Europe and Southeast Asia came about is also the story of how it ended.

We have already explored in some detail the question of why the United States did not turn fascist. It was clearly not a question of the ruling class opting for democracy over fascist dictatorship. White supremacy and Hitler's doctrine of the "master race" was as much an American phenomenon as it was German.

Consequently, when fascism was on the rise in Tokyo, Rome and Berlin and perpetrating acts of aggression in China, Ethiopia, Spain and Poland, the U.S. government as a matter of policy did nothing to stop its rise.

When Mussolini invaded Ethiopia in 1935 American capitalists were not prevented from supplying Italy with huge quantities of oil despite a declared embargo by the U.S. government. When Hitler and Mussolini

---

24 "Manifesto of the Communist International to the Workers of the World," quoted in Leon Trotsky, *The First 5 Years of the Communist International* (Monad Press, 1972), 25.

supported the fascist rebellion in Spain against a democratically-elected government, President Roosevelt did nothing but shut off help by declaring neutrality.

The pillars holding up the fascist movement were anti-communism and racism/national chauvinism. So long as the spearhead of fascism was anti-communism, the ruling classes of Europe and America were complicit and did not lift a finger to stop the mass murdering of Jews, communists, workers, gay/lesbian/transgender people and the Romani people. This wavering in the face of fascist aggressions helped unleash a World War that cost humanity over 80 million lives. Twenty-seven million of those lives were taken as a result of Hitler's invasion of the Soviet Union.

The attack on Pearl Harbor on December 7, 1941 was declared by President Roosevelt as a day of infamy, but in 1937 the Japanese imperialists' all-out invasion of China and their slaughtering of millions was no cause for U.S. outrage. Obviously, the United States entered the war to save its own well-established empire in the South Pacific and not out of respect or in solidarity with the victims of Japanese imperialism or to end the control of some nations over others.

World War II was not a "white man's war" fought out in a European theater but a worldwide war that started also in China and Ethiopia. It was a worldwide struggle of workers, colonial slaves and nationally oppressed peoples against the Axis slave powers of European and Japanese imperialism. Thus, victory over the fascists marked an unprecedented historic advance of the anti-imperialist, democratic peoples of the world. The system of colonial oppression which had been the fundamental cause of this world war was shaken and showed signs of collapsing and being routed by communist/democratically-led national liberation movements, particularly in China, Vietnam, Indonesia and the Philippines. Along with the liberated countries of Eastern Europe, there also emerged in Asia a new block of socialist-led liberated countries.

The colonially and nationally-oppressed of Africa quickly perceived this new balance of forces in the world to be in favor of national liberation; they quickly understood that now was the time to raise the cry of "Africa for Africans." And not only was this cry raised in Africa but throughout the world where Africans had been enslaved.

9

The Question of Black Liberation and the
Struggle Against Imperialism: Post-World War II Era

Harry Haywood wrote his book, *Negro Liberation,* in 1948. The war was over, and in its wake, there emerged a socialist block of nations led by the Soviet Union, an undisputed friend and ally of the colonial slaves of Africa and Asia and Black people in America. Haywood's opening remarks in his book reads like a warning, said he: "The American Negro faces the most crucial decision in his entire history. All of the gains so powerfully won by him through years of struggle and sacrifice stand in jeopardy as the specter of World War II looms sinisterly above the skyscrapers of Wall Street."[1]

In order to see precisely why Black people were confronted with this "most crucial decision" let us quickly review the worldwide situation of the colonized peoples and the realignment of the imperialist powers after the war.

The old colonial empires of Europe, particularly the German, British and French empires, where shaken to their foundations by World War II. In 1945 W.E.B. Du Bois, the intellectual forebearer of the Civil Rights movement of the 20th century, put this cataclysmic collapse of European culture in historical perspective in a booklet entitled *Color and Democracy: Colonies and Peace.*[2]

Like Marx and Engels in the *Communist Manifesto,* Du Bois acknowledges the expansion of Europe in terms of the phenomenal development of physical science, invention, technology and the efficiency of capitalist production. Urbanization, the increase in population, the migration of entire populations due to improved mass transportation and new techniques of communication undeniably brought with it the development of rational

---

1   Haywood, *Negro Liberation,* 5.
2   W. E. B. Du Bois, *Color and Democracy: Colonies and Peace* (Harcourt Brace & Co., 1945).

thinking, practical and secular points of view. Indeed, these civilizational changes constituted real benefits in all areas of the world. But benefits for whom and to what end? These civilizational changes were not without catastrophic consequences for people not socially and economically developed enough to understand and technologically too weak to resist European expansion.

Before the Holocaust of World War II in Europe, there was the extermination of indigenous populations, the devastation wrought by the African slave trade, the endless wars of conquest in Africa, the Americas and Asia that carried in their wake endless human misery and genocide. Long before the carnage of war in Europe and the decimation of its populations there was the long period of colonial wars stretching from the 15th century to the 20th century. As Aime Cesaire put it in his essay *On Colonialism*, Hitler "...applied to Europe colonialist procedures which until then had been reserved exclusively for the Arabs of Algeria, the 'coolies' of India and the 'niggers' of Africa."[3]

Dr. W.E.B. Du Bois, speaking on the founding of the United Nations in 1944, and its failure to recognize the color line and the colonized nations' right to self-determination, did not neglect to mention his own people who exist as an oppressed nation within the United States. It was "...left to the greatest modern democracy, the United States," Du Bois wrote, "to defend human slavery and caste, and even defeat democratic government in its own borders, ostensibly because of an inferior race, but really to make profits out of cheap labor, both black and white."[4]

Once again, the pseudo-humanism of imperialism was manifested, as narrow, fragmented, chauvinistic and racist. And of course, the colonial peoples of the world were the first to see this and rebel against these new dangers to world peace, these thinly veiled attempts to build a new world order based on continued enslavement and oppression.

Into this is the new world order, declared and institutionalized by the United Nations, the North Atlantic Treaty Organization (NATO) and the South East Asia Treaty Organization (SEATO), the United States summoned Gunnar Myrdal, Swedish sociologist, economist and social democrat, to serve and provide the ideological props for understanding the "Negro Problem" in America.

After the war, the United States emerged as a world power, a new imperialist master towering over the semi-colonial millions of Africa, Asia and Latin America. With national liberation movements, this meant that

---

3   Aimé Césaire, *Discourse on Colonialism* (Monthly Review Press, 2001), 36.
4   Du Bois, *Color and Democracy*, 85.

the U.S would present itself as the "friend" of those nations seeking independence from their colonial masters in Europe. And those nations wondered, "How can you be our friend while you are denying 20 million Black people the most elementary rights of democracy?"

What was then called "The Negro Problem" in the U.S. had the obvious potential of exposing the U.S. monopoly-capitalists as the new reactionary center of Western imperialism. Given this reality the national question regarding Black people in the United States was of the greatest importance and there was the need to clarify where Black people stood in the worldwide struggle against imperialism. Both the ruling class, the communists and the Black Liberation movement sharply felt the need to examine the problem anew and to set forth a program of action.

Let us first deal with the ruling class response to the earth-shaking anti-imperialist movements springing up all over the world and their program of action.

The U.S. ruling class did not summon Du Bois, Carter G. Woodson, E. Franklin Frazier or any of that whole battalion of Black scholars who had made the study of Black life and culture their lifetime pursuit. No, instead in the name of "scientific objectivity" the ruling class summoned Gunnar Myrdal and granted him the financial resources to pull together Black and white scholars in an historically unprecedented scholarly enterprise designed to exhaustively study and analyze the "Negro Problem."

In the fall of 2004, Professor Shari Cohen, writing in *Carnegie Results*, states:

> Gunnar Myrdal's *An American Dilemma: The Negro Problem and Modern Democracy*, generally viewed as one of the most important results of grantmaking by Carnegie Corporation of New York, played a major role in the story that led from an America, which after World War II still had a legal Jim Crow system in the South—along with a segregated army—to the Voting Rights Act of 1965. It was cited as the social scientific evidence justifying the Supreme Court's decision that what had been deemed separate but equal education for black children was, in fact, detrimental to their development.
>
> Published in 1944 (by Harper & Bros.; reprinted in 1996 by Transaction Publishers), *An American Dilemma* served to crystallize the emerging awareness that racial discrimination and legal segregation could not endure in the U.S. Its moral wake-up call for Americans to live up to the democratic ideals of the 'American Creed became a powerful justification that united the major groups responsible for the civil rights movement. It has been called one of the most important works of social science of the twentieth century. Never before had so comprehensive and wide-

ranging a study of the state of black Americans and interracial relations been carried out.[5]

This particular summation of Myrdal's work and its impact on the struggle against racial segregation or the Civil Rights movement clearly demonstrates it was intended as a "moral wake-up for America" to live up to its "democratic ideals" and to make good its declaration that all are equal and endowed with certain inalienable rights. The "Negro Problem" in America was posited as a moral crisis and Myrdal provided the scientific evidence within the framework of bourgeois ideology. Bourgeois ideology sees capitalism as the end of history rather than turning to a new page in human development.

It seems like everyone, every leading Black thinker or academic praised Myrdal's book as a monumental contribution to scientifically understanding "The Negro Problem." There were, however, exceptions like Oliver Cromwell Cox. Cox's position is summarized here by Adolph Reed:

> *An American Dilemma*, the most exhaustive survey of race relations ever undertaken in the United States, is for the most part a useful source of data. In detail it presents many ingenious analyses of the materials. But it develops no hypothesis or consistent theory of race relations; and, to the extent that it employs the caste belief in interpretations, it is misleading. Clearly, the use of "the American Creed" as the "value premise" for his study severely limits and narrows Dr. Myrdal's perspective. Even though we should grant some right of the author to limit the discussion of his subject to its moral aspects, he still develops it without insight. He never brings into focus the two great systems of morality currently striving in our civilization for ascendancy, but merely assumes a teleological abstraction of social justice toward which all good men will ultimately gravitate. Moreover, since we can hardly accuse him of being naïve, and since he clearly goes out of his way to avoid the obvious implications of labor exploitation in the South, we cannot help concluding that the work in many respects may have the effect of a powerful piece of propaganda in favor of the status quo. If the "race problem" in the United States is preeminently a moral question, it must naturally be resolved by moral means, and this conclusion is precisely the social illusion which the ruling political class has constantly sought to produce.[6]

---

5   Shari Cohen, "The Lasting Legacy of An American Dilemma," *Carnegie Results* (Carnegie Corporation of New York, 2004), accessed on December 11, 2020, https://www.carnegie.org/publications/lasting-legacy-american-dilemma/.

6   Reed, "Race and Class in the Work of Oliver Cromwell Cox."

And what are "the two great systems of morality striving in our civilization for ascendancy"? They are the system of morality based on capitalism and the system of morality based on socialism.

Now let us deal with the question of Black liberation, or what Harry Haywood called "Negro liberation."

Clearly the war against fascism left its mark on Black people in the United States, and especially Black soldiers coming home. Now that the German, Italian and Japanese fascists were defeated, now that the fascists were driven from the battlefields of war by the heroic people in colonized countries, the Soviet Union, China, North Africa and the Pacific realm and by the nationally oppressed peoples of the world, still, the Black soldiers returning home had to contend with Jim Crow, with being lynched, discriminated against and denied the right to vote.

The ruling-class barons of Wall Street and their political hacks in Washington D.C. knew about Jim Crow and the problems it posed for U.S. hegemony in the wake of World War II. That is precisely why Gunnar Myrdal was sought out to advance the notion that the "Negro Problem" was not a problem of national liberation or self-determination but exclusively a civil rights problem to be resolved by appealing to the "American Creed" or the moral conscience of the ruling class.

Harry Haywood, representing the view of the Communist Party USA at the time, saw matters differently. For Haywood, the enemy was not simply ideas of racial superiority tramped in the minds of white people, but institutionalized racism perpetrated by a Nazi-like system of Jim Crow.

Haywood recognized the historic advance made by the defeat of the "Axis slave powers" in Berlin, Rome and Tokyo. The crack in the imperialist system made by this advance stretched all the way from India, China and the Pacific realm to Eastern Europe, Italy and North Africa. There existed this objective state of affairs, along with the emergence of a socialist bloc of nations that was friendly to the cause of Black liberation. This new international alignment of the Soviet Union and developing countries objectively helped to strengthen the Black Liberation `movement in the U.S. and Africa.

But similarly, the defeat of fascism and the rising tide of anti-imperialism was also the basis for a new resolve on the part of monopoly capitalists to stem the tide of liberation. The resurgence of reaction and a neo-fascist movement was now being driven by a handful of greedy Wall Street monopolists. They saw an opportunity to seize the spoils of the fallen empires of Europe and re-enslave the colonized nations and semi-dependencies under the banner of "freedom and democracy" fashioned by Henry Luce's concept of an "American Century." Luce, the son of a missionary, came out in 1941 in an article in *Life* magazine calling upon the United States to abandon its "isolationism" and become the "Good Samaritan" spreading "democracy and freedom" in a world devastated and shattered by war. Luce was the flip side of Gunnar Myrdal, wherein Luce wanted to export the idealized "American Creed" and Myrdal wanted to make it the driving force of democracy at home and key to solving the "Negro Problem." Luce projected that American ideals would "...do their mysterious work of lifting the life of mankind from the level of the beast to what the Psalmist called a little lower than the angels."

Haywood correctly characterized these proclamations as "sinister aims" and "hypocritical use of the slogans of freedom and democracy." Pursuant to their profit-hungry stance the Wall Street imperialists whipped up an anti-communist crusade and hysteria to cloak their program of expansionism and imperialist aggression. They promised free elections and democracy to the world but dare not have one in Mississippi. To have free, democratic elections in the Southern states would have been a betrayal of the Wall Street alliance with the bourbon planters of the South.

President Truman gave lip service to civil rights at home while carrying out a program of subverting democracy abroad. This was the American Dilemma: being a champion and saboteur of democracy at the same time. And the blatant denial of the rights of Black people historically rooted in vestiges of chattel slavery is the driving contradiction of this dilemma. But as Haywood put it, Black people in the U.S.A. were not "...ignorant to the fact that among the warmest supporters of the 'new crusade' for world 'emancipation' are the most vicious poll taxers and Negrophobes of the whole country..."[7]

The ruling class acknowledged that there was indeed a "Negro Problem," but unlike Harry Haywood they chose not to see it as a problem of national oppression requiring for its solution the demands of the Negro Liberation movement for self-determination and social, economic and political equality.

Seen as a problem of national oppression, after World War II and historically, "The Negro Question," according to Haywood is "agrarian in origin. It involves the problem of a depressed peasantry living under a system of sharecropping, riding-boss supervision, debt slavery, chronic land hunger and dependency—the plantation, a relic of chattel slavery."[8]

---

7   Haywood, *Negro Liberation*, 6.
8   Haywood, *Negro Liberation*, 11.

The American Dilemma that Haywood sees is the "...curious anomaly of a virtual serfdom in the very heart of the most industrialized country in the world. Slave-whipping barbarism at the center of 'enlightened' twentieth-century capitalist culture—that is the core of America's 'race' problem".[9]

In 1948, when Haywood wrote *Negro Liberation*, there were about 80,000 members in the Communist Party, 14% of them being Black, 46% industrial workers, 46% women and 25% professional white-collar workers.

In 1943, Benjamin J. Davis, Jr. had been elected as the first Black communist to the New York City Council.

With the Communist Party USA still being a force to be reckoned with, one could not think of a better historical moment to present, from a revolutionary point of view, the question of Black liberation as a national question. With the revolutionary upheavals in Eastern Europe and China and the emerging struggles for national liberation in the African colonies, this would seemingly be the best possible time to link the struggle for Black Liberation with the worldwide independence movements of colonies and the emerging socialist bloc of nations.

Yes, it was an idyllic moment, except for a few nagging contradictions. One of these contradictions was the attempt of Communist Party leader, Earl Browder, to ideologically betray and liquidate the Communist Party. Browder proposed that the U.S. working class help Wall Street grab world trade as a precondition for assuring the peace in a war-torn world. In the words of William Z. Foster:

> Browder's scheme was a crass revision of Marxism-Leninism. In his...thesis he obliterated the class struggle, overcame the basic contradictions of capitalism, eliminated the conception of imperialism (the very word 'imperialism' became taboo to him), and did away with the perspective of socialism.[10]

What did this lack of a socialist perspective mean in terms of policy? It meant betrayal of national liberation struggles abroad and at home, putting 4,000 foreign-born members out of the Communist Party, eliminating shop groups, abdicating the leading role of the working class and the party, and glorifying the "progressive role" of U.S. monopoly capitalism.

This revisionist line, authored and implemented by Browder and his faction, weakened and destroyed the mass work of the party. It took the

---

9   Haywood, *Negro Liberation*, 11.
10   Foster, *History of the Communist Party*, 426.

position, ignoring over a century of Black history, that the masses of Black people had abandoned their national aspirations and were now integrated into the white population.

In brief, when Haywood wrote *Negro Liberation* in 1948, the communist work in the South had practically been liquidated under Browderism. Haywood's brilliant exposition on the question did not do away with the damage done.

Nevertheless, even though the ruling class and the revisionists have to this day denied the existence of national oppression in the United States, we think the thesis set forth in *Negro Liberation* is basically correct. In order to demonstrate this, we must examine Haywood's thesis in the light of new statistical data and socio-economic developments.

What is a nation?

Stalin thus defines a nation:

> "A nation is a historically constituted, stable community of people, formed on the basis of a common language, territory, economic life, and psychological make-up manifested in a common culture."[11]

Presentation of the Problem

We have already essayed about how Harry Haywood described the question of a Black Nation being agrarian in origin. In 1948 this meant that the problem of Black people was that of a depressed, landless peasant population living under a system of sharecropping, debt slavery, hunger and dependency. In other words, the plantation system created during chattel slavery and existing as a relic of slavery was the problem.

That was the problem in 1948. Is it the problem now in 2021? Due to about 100 years of out-migration from the South, expansion of industries in the South and increased urbanization of Black people, the configuration of the problem has changed. But the problem of Black people being an oppressed nation has not changed, hence, the struggle for Black Liberation continues.

What does the Black Belt, the physical location of the Black nation, look like today?

---

11   Joseph Stalin, "Marxism and the National Question," *Collected Works*, vol. 2 (Foreign Languages Publishing House, 1953), accessed on December 11, 2020, https://www.marxists.org/reference/archive/stalin/works/1913/03a.htm.

According to the 2010 U.S. Census, 42 million Black people live in the United States, making up 14% of the total population. The proportion of the population that is Black has not changed since 1900.

The ten states with the largest Black populations are:

District of Columbia	50.7%	(305,125)
Mississippi	37.3%	(1,098,385)
Louisiana	32.4%	(1,452,396)
Georgia	30.5%	(2,950,435)
Maryland	29.4%	(1,700,298)
South Carolina	27.9%	(1,290,684)
Alabama	26.2%	(1,251,311)
North Carolina	21.5%	(2,048,628)
Delaware	21.4%	(191,551)
Virginia	19.4%	(1,390,293)

The South has the highest percentage of Black people (57% according to the 2010 U.S. Census) and the Black Belt region of the South has the highest concentration of Black people. This Black Belt region and its boundaries is a band through the center of the deep South, but also stretching as far north as Delaware and as far west as east Texas.

The political use of the term "Black Belt" designates the counties where the Black population constitutes a majority. From the 1940s to the present the Black Belt comprises about 200 counties forming a crescent from Virginia to Texas.

The U.S. Census Report in 2000 identified 96 counties in the United States with Black populations of more than 50%. 95 of the counties are located across the coastal and lowland South in a loose arc related to the traditional Black Belt region embracing the Mississippi Delta.

In 2000 the U.S. Department of Agriculture proposed creating a federal regional commission similar to the Appalachian Regional Commission to address the social economic problems of the Black Belt. And what precisely are those problems?

Low educational attainment, poor health care, high infant mortality rates, substandard housing, massive unemployment and high crime rates. Historically this region has experienced lack of economic development. This backwardness disproportionally affects Black people and the working poor, therefore affecting all who live in this region.

In 1948 when Haywood describes the Black Belt as a depressed area bearing the legacy of chattel slavery he could have very well been speaking about today. This region is still the core of the U.S. race problem and constitutes the objective material basis of the national oppression of Black people.

In the past, both communist and some Black revolutionary nationalists have considered the Black Belt as the national territory of Black people within the United States. The National Movement for the Establishment of a 49th State, founded by Chicago businessman Oscar Brown, Sr., saw the South as home of the Black Nation. Similarly, The Republic of New Afrika has identified the Black Belt as the land base for the Black Nation and militantly advocates for the right of self-determination and independence.[12]

In the 1930s the Communist Party's program recognized the struggle for Black Liberation and the right of self-determination in the Black Belt. As we have noted above it was during this period that the Party organized the Sharecroppers Union and led militant union organizing while at the same time challenging Jim Crow and its system of legalized lynching. The Sharecroppers Union in Alabama had thousands of members in 73 locals, 80 women's auxiliaries and 30 youth groups. The Sharecroppers Union led the first organized strike of agricultural workers in the deep South. In 1930 about 500 people populated the Party's mass organizations; between 80% and 90% were Black people. Also, in 1930 the communists did what no political party had done since Black Reconstruction, they endorsed Walter Lewis, a Black candidate, for governor of Alabama.[13]

It was not by some ingenious device for recruiting or brilliant propaganda strategy that the Communist Party gained so much ground with Black people in the deep South. Communists gained so much ground because they were programmatically and concretely addressing the most elemental demands of the struggle for Black Liberation. One, they recognized the existence of the Black Nation, its inalienable democratic right to determine its own political destiny. And two, they joined in the class struggle and the struggle for Black Liberation on the ground, at the grassroots level. Such is the great lesson we must cull from this very rich period of struggle from 1930 to 1941. A period, by the way, that laid the foundations for the emerging Civil Rights movement of the 1950s and 60s, which in its turn became the indispensable precondition for the Black Liberation movement today.

---

12 Ajamu Nangwaya and Kali Akuno, eds., *Jackson Rising: The Struggle for Economic Democracy and Black Self-determination in Jackson, Mississippi* (Daraja Press, 2017).
13 Kelley, *Hammer and Hoe*, 16-17.

10

Seeing the Present in the Candid Light of the Past

There was an historical rumor afloat in the late 1960s that Henry Kissinger once asked Chou En-lai, a great communist leader of China, what he thought of the French Revolution and his answer was: "It's too soon to tell." True that. Even though revolutions constitute sudden and catastrophic breaks in the continuum of human history, the revolutionary process itself, driven by the dynamics of internecine class warfare, is a long and protracted process that consumes entire generations. So, the question of how we use the past to cast the more candid light of truth upon the present is an important one. And as Marxist-Leninists we believe this is what we must always be doing; we must apply the lessons of history in order to wage effective struggles in the present.

Lenin correctly pointed out:

> Every revolution means a sharp turn in the lives of a vast number of people. Unless the time is ripe for such a turn, no real revolution can take place. And just as any turn in the life of an individual teaches him a great deal and brings rich experience and great emotional stress, so a revolution teaches an entire people very rich and valuable lessons in a short space of time.[1]

In other words, we live in a revolutionary era, more so than all the previous eras of history, where the masses apply and learn the lessons of history in the very moment when they are making history. The struggle for Black Liberation and socialism is an ongoing struggle that must and does draw valuable lessons from the history of our movement and our revolutionary traditions.

---

1   Lenin, "Lessons of the Revolution," in *Collected Works*, vol. 25, accessed on December 18, 2020, https://www.marxists.org/archive/lenin/works/1917/sep/06.htm.

But before we can draw lessons, there are certain facts about our history that must be assessed. And what we have endeavored to accomplish here is to demonstrate that, given the objective reality of capitalism and its contradictory development, from the very beginning the struggle for Black Liberation and socialism have been organically related.

Marx not only gave a correct economic analysis of the relationship between capitalism and slavery, he went further and drew the unmistakable conclusion that the white portion of the working class cannot be free if Black portion is branded, bought and sold. He pointed out that the direct slavery in colonies throughout the world was a pedestal for wage-slavery in the industrial centers of Europe. The posing of the tasks of the international working class in the battle against slavery and colonial oppression in this manner made the battle an indispensable precondition of the self-emancipation of the working class. This was and is the revolutionary essence of Marxism. Marx did not simply make a brilliant observation that slavery created the financial basis for the industrial revolution. He also stated repeatedly that the abolition of slavery was a necessary precondition for the self-emancipation of the working class. Marx and Engels, the founders of scientific socialism and the Communist Party, believed that the struggle against slavery was central to the struggle against capitalism and for socialism.

Marx also saw the struggle against colonialism in a similar light. In 1853, he wrote in the *New York Daily Tribune*: "The profound hypocrisy and inherent barbarism of bourgeois civilization lies unveiled before our eyes, turning from its home, where it assumes respectable forms, to the colonies where it goes naked."[2]

In these United States we are duty bound to reassert and fight for this revolutionary essence of Marxism to be acknowledged and accepted. We must, as I have tried to demonstrate herein above, affirm the facts of history, which clearly show that the social democrats of the Second International betrayed the very essence of Marxism when they maintained that there was no "Negro Question." Thus, Lenin and the Third International exposed this betrayal and restored that revolutionary essence of Marxism, which recognizes the national and colonial question as being central to the historic tasks of winning the struggle for socialism.

In the summer of 1930 when hunger was stalking the land like a beast of prey, the Communist Party organized Unemployed Councils across the country that were grassroots and locally based. In the Deep South, going

---

2   Karl Marx, quoted in Robin D. G. Kelley, *Freedom Dreams: The Black Radical Imagination* (Beacon Press, 2002), 40.

up against the police and KKK mobs, the party organized councils under the slogan "United we eat." Organizers, both Black and white, lived off starvation wages and under the constant threat of death. But Black people, especially Black workers and peasants, were ready to fight and so, according to communist organizer Otto Hall, by April 3, 1930 "nearly a thousand Negroes joined the party."[3]

Figure 12 — Communist leaders and Smith Act defendants (from left) William Z. Foster, Benjamin Davis, Eugene Dennis, Henry Winston, Robert Thompson and Jack Stachel. Starting in 1949, the U.S. government tried to outlaw the Communist Party with the unconstitutional Smith Act. This came right on the heels of Earl Browder and his faction's attempt to liquidate the party.

In the 1930s and up until the opening shots of World War II, the Black Liberation movement and the movement for socialism merged in the Deep, Black Belt South to make the glorious history that many post-Cold War scholars, like Gilmore, Kelley, and Gerald Horne talk about in their great academic studies. The historic accomplishments of U.S. communists and the Communist International is acknowledged even to the point of admitting the red roots of the Civil Rights movement—but then comes a

---

3   Gilmore, *Defying Dixie*, 113.

peculiar anti-communist/anti-Black people twist that I have directly addressed in this book. The twist is this: that the idea of nationhood, and the national consciousness yearning for national liberation was imposed on Black people via the Communist International as opposed to it coming organically from the struggle against chattel slavery and its 20th century vestiges in the institutionalizing of Jim Crow.

This was a Cold War lie manufactured by the monopoly capitalists in the wake of World War II. This lie was part and parcel of the repression that began with Senator Martin Dies in Texas, continued after the 1947 declaration of the Truman Doctrine, and culminated in the Foley Square trials of communists in New York City in 1949. In pursuit of the communist foe, the ideals of bourgeois democracy, allegedly enshrined in the Bill of Rights of the Constitution, were hastily cast aside. Harry Haywood, representing the Communist Party USA, responded to this lie and the Cold War mythmakers when he wrote the book *Negro Liberation*.

Epilogue

As we pointed out in the introduction to this historical essay, our objective is confined to discussing and assessing the role of the Communist Party USA in building a strategic alliance between the multinational working-class movement and the struggle for Black Liberation. Having completed this task, more or less, we must now address how all this relates to the present.

Let us return for a moment to the nature of the national question with respect to Black people. In the detailed historical review, we have given above, we saw that the Communist Party in the United States came into the Communist International movement with the position that Black people were neither a "colonial people" nor a "nation," but simply a race. This formulation was rejected by the Communist International as being superficial, because by defining the so-called "Negro problem" as a race problem, one fails to recognize the special characteristics of the oppression of Black people that gives the struggle for Black Liberation its national quality.

When we say Black people in the U.S. constitute a nation, we mean more than what is usually meant by nation. We take our lead from the Black Liberation movement going back to Martin R. Delany and, just as important, from the *Theses of the Second Congress of the Communist International*, which states, in part, that "The Communist Party...must base its policy on the national question, too, not on abstract principles, but first, on a precise appraisal of the historic situation, and primarily on economic conditions."[1]

According to the 1920 U.S. Census, 86.1% out of 12 million Black people lived in the South and over 66% of them were landless peasants, earning their livelihood from various agricultural occupations, but mostly sharecropping. In this particular moment of history, the Black population was concentrated in the Black Belt, which stretched from Delaware through all the Southern states to East Texas. It is clear from the historical facts we've already presented hereinabove that in 1928 the communists were correct in pointing out that, given the economic foundations of

---

1   Allen and Foner, *American Communism*, 173.

racism and the social and political relationships arising from this, that even before the Civil War, Black people came to see themselves as a nation and developed characteristic traits of an oppressed nationality within the United States.

In 1947, 82 years after the Civil War ended, the NAACP issued an "Appeal to the World" through the United Nations in which they declared that: "Prolonged policies of segregation and discrimination have involuntarily welded the mass almost into a nation within a nation with its own schools, churches, hospitals, newspapers and many business enterprises."[2]

What happened after the Civil War was that, even though slavery was abolished, Black people, due to the counter-revolutionary overthrow of Black Reconstruction, were rendered landless peasants, forced to return to the plantations as sharecroppers and denied every semblance of political empowerment although they were a majority in over 90 Black Belt counties. Despite the massive out-migration to the North in search of jobs, the proletarianization that started in the 1920s and 30s, and the mechanization that displaced Black agricultural workers in the 1950s, the basic national character of Black people remained.

During World War II, while the South was being industrialized, especially in Alabama, still the great majority of Black people lived in the South under the iron heel of institutionalized racism (i.e., Jim Crow) enforcing a system of sharecropping and debt peonage. The semi-feudal character of this exploitation existed side-by-side with highly developed forms of capitalist exploitation in the textile mills of North Carolina, the steel mills of Alabama, and the coal mines stretching from western Pennsylvania, West Virginia, eastern Kentucky and to southern Illinois.

The vestiges of slavery were strongly embedded in this newly emerged situation of economic and social inequality arising out of the unfinished revolution of 1861-1877. Clearly the roots of the national oppression of Black people was in the South and it was a question of landless peasants existing as a half-enslaved people under pre-capitalist forms of exploitation enforced by a system of state-sanctioned violence involving lynch mobs, police terror and penal slavery via jails, prison farms and prisons.

Fundamentally, Black people lived in the agrarian countryside of the South and in separate and segregated quarters of the South and North. In some Southern cities, Black people also lived in what is called the "old slave quarters" (e.g. Vine City in Atlanta, Georgia or the Northeast section of Washington DC). The vestiges of slavery still exist but there have been important quantitative and qualitative changes in the class composition of

---

2   Foster, *The Negro People*, 468.

Black people, due to both increased industrialization and the mechanization of agriculture in the South.

In the 1930s the Communist Party position was "It is impossible to solve the Negro question without freeing the half-enslaved population of the South from the pre-capitalist forms of exploitation. This task, naturally, can be performed only by the proletarian revolution."[3] This position, based on the then existing objective conditions and class relations, was consistent with the basic teachings of Marx summarized in the expression that labor in a white skin cannot be free if it is branded and sold in a Black skin or denied full citizenship rights.

Based on this historically determined reality we draw the following conclusions:

1. The fight for Black Liberation in fact still has a national character. While the semi-feudal relations of property in the South served as a condition for the development of the Black nation, the fact that most African Americans are now workers does not mean that Blacks as a distinct nationality have ceased to exist or that there is no national oppression—just as the people of Ireland and Palestine face national oppression.

2. The fact that more Black people became workers strengthened the Black Liberation movement as a multi-class movement. A rigorous, scientific assessment of the role of the Black proletariat in the Black Liberation movement settles the question of which class must lead this movement. Nonetheless, as Marxist-Leninists, we must continue to struggle for the leadership of the working class.

3. What makes the experience of the 1930s so important and vital to our movement today is that it laid the basis, both practically and theoretically, for building a strategic alliance in the united front against monopoly capitalism rooted in the struggle against the national oppression of Black people. For if history has taught anything, then it must be the building of a strategic alliance between the national liberation movements in our country and the multinational working class. However, a key to building such an alliance is the recognition of the centrality of the struggle for Black Liberation in the struggle for socialism in these United States of America.

This is where I would have ended this book but for the fact that the largest Black-led rebellion in U.S. history occurred in May 2020.

---

3   Allen and Foner, *American Communism*, 174.

The Unfinished Revolution and Black Rebellion Today

Before speaking directly on the May Rebellion of 2020 let us first provide the historical context by once again reviewing some of the main points in our book in order to cast a more candid light on the unfolding of present events.

War, as the saying goes, is the midwife of revolution, but the Civil War was the revolution. Once the Union soldiers set foot in the South, slaves started what Du Bois appropriately called "The General Strike." This was the first lethal blow against chattel slavery delivered by the slaves themselves. More precisely, in the words of Du Bois, "...with perplexed and laggard steps, the United States government followed in the footsteps of the black slave."[4] The North responded to the treacherous act of war perpetrated by the South with a war to save the Union and the slaves responded with open rebellion. It was reported that on the Magnolia Plantation in Louisiana not only did Black people refuse to work but proceeded to erect gallows in the slave quarters because they believed they must hang their masters to be free. Black people, despite Lincoln, made the Civil War a war against slavery by their revolutionary deeds.

At the conclusion of his monumental work *Black Reconstruction* W.E.B. Du Bois observed: "...the slave went free; stood a brief moment in the sun; then moved back again toward slavery."[5] That is, was "moved back toward slavery" by the terror and violence unleashed by counter-revolution. A counter-revolution so mean-spirited, and so driven by the Southern bourbons of white supremacy that it sought to erase from history books and history the great historical achievements of Black people in the most earth-shaking revolution of the 19th century, ending the South's un holy crusade against labor.

All revolutions have enduring accomplishments. Counter-revolutions, no matter how thorough and reactionary they are, can only retard, distort and stall the revolutionary process. They cannot stop the revolutionary process.

So, what were the enduring accomplishments of the Civil War that set the stage for Radical Reconstruction then and a large part of the strategy for Black liberation now? It was adding the Thirteenth, Fourteenth and Fifteenth Amendments to the U.S. Constitution which respectively abolished chattel slavery (the liquidation of property in human beings),

---

4   Du Bois, quoted in Eric Foner, *Reconstruction: America's Unfinished Revolution*, 1863-1877 (Harper, 2011), 4.

5   Du Bois, *Black Reconstruction*, 30.

provided equal protection of the law, making citizenship a birthright, and guaranteed the right to vote. In addition to these amendments, the federal statutes[6] which created an enforcement mechanism for the rights of citizenship, have been the basic enduring revolutionary accomplishments of the Civil War and Reconstruction era.

From the short-lived political revolution of Black Reconstruction to the present, the enduring accomplishments of the Civil War that ended chattel slavery and opened the radical era of Black Reconstruction have haunted the movement for Black Liberation. Every movement that has taken root with the masses of Black people has had to do with Black self-determination and the rights denied us as citizens, i.e., the freedoms that were halfheartedly given but wholeheartedly taken away with the end of Reconstruction. Whether we are in the turn of the century in 1900, the 1920s, 30s, 40s, 50s, 60s or the present, the cry has been for freedom, justice and equality, for the full restoration of those citizenship rights and privileges we were granted by Congress.

We have been left this particular legacy of struggle because, in the wake of the counter-revolution that ended Reconstruction and established a reign of terror, a system of dual sovereignty, whereby the Southern states under the banner of the old Confederate flag (the stars and bars) were granted the right by executive fiat and judicial decrees to legally set up a regime of racist oppression, political repression of Black people was established. This system, which came to be known as Jim Crow, was blatantly enforced by lynch-mob terror and was a police-state apparatus designed to control segregated Black communities in the South and throughout the nation.

We submit that the mass, Black-led rebellion that started in response to the murder of George Floyd, Breonna Taylor and others occurred within the historical context outlined hereinabove and throughout this book. And, that it must be examined from the standpoint of this historic tension created by the denial of equality and the national oppression of Black people, because this is the driving contradiction of every Black-led rebellion since the birth of this nation. Civil rights and especially the right to vote have been historically suppressed to keep Black people oppressed. The great rebellion of May 2020 was not just a moment of outrage over the murders of George Floyd, Breonna Taylor and others, it was a clarion call for freedom, justice and equality; a manifesto coming from the masses

---

6   United States Code, Title 42, Chapter 21, Subchapter 1, secs. 1981-1985, accessed on January 28, 2021, https://uscode.house.gov/browse/prelim@title42/chapter21/subchapter1&edition=prelim.

in the streets. The placards in the street protests carried messages of defiance. One said, "Resist fear, we are many—they are few," and another read, "Our enslaved labor built this nation—we can end it."

We are now in a phase of struggle which some, like the Reverend Dr. William Barber of North Carolina, would characterize as a struggle for the Third Reconstruction. We think it is deeper, we think it is the youth sounding the death knell of the racist police repression that stands like a blockade in the road to Black liberation. It is a call for mass resistance to the police terror that has stalked our communities and denied us the organizing space we need as a nationally oppressed people to wage the struggle for Black Liberation, to finish the unfinished revolution.

We are in a pandemic where over two people a minute are dying from COVID-19. Disproportionately most of the people dying are Black, due to the wretched conditions of poverty, homelessness, poor health care services and massive unemployment. The social unrest agitated by these conditions is being addressed with racist repression and police tyranny. These are the material conditions that gave rise to the Black-led May 2020 rebellion, where 26 million people protested and took to the streets in all 50 states of the United States.

However, the importance of the working-class character of the Rebellion must be emphasized. In Chicago, Minneapolis, St. Louis, Baltimore, Jacksonville, Tallahassee, Detroit, Atlanta, Portland and many other urban centers of resistance, hundreds of thousands (perhaps even millions) of white workers participated in this Black-led uprising. The COVID-19 pandemic and the economic devastation that follows in its wake has exposed the fact that racism offers no material benefits or privileges to the millions of white workers living in poverty and suffering from massive unemployment. To be sure what is really going on is that the present crisis in health care and economics has spawned the economic conditions (like in the 1930s) that will unite workers on the picket lines and in their respective communities and enable them to find common ground in the struggle against national oppression and monopoly capitalism.

The End for Then, a New Beginning for Now

We believe that now we stand in the rosy dawn of a new movement to finally finish the unfinished revolution that was the Civil War of 1861.

Since the overthrow of Reconstruction, i.e., the ending by violence and terror the revolutionary gains of the Civil War, there is a whole other history of alliances and compromises between the old former slaveholding South and the high-finance Northern capitalists to continue the oppression and super-exploitation of Black people. The Thirteenth, Fourteenth and Fifteenth Amendments to the U.S. Constitution abolishing slavery, granting citizenship as a birth right, equal protection of rights and the right to vote were kept on paper but not fully enforced even 'til this day.

This is not 1861. This is 2021, but we live in the shadow of the unfinished revolution started by the last Civil War. To go forward, we believe Black people, united with class-conscious workers and Marxist-Leninists, must muster the masses, firmly and unequivocally putting forth an agenda for Black and brown liberation and a class-struggle agenda for hundreds of millions of workers who are dying and suffering from this pandemic health crisis and economic devastation leaving in its wake millions unemployed stuck in dire poverty.

Figures

1. Legg, Frank W. "Frederick Douglass." *Frank W. Legg Photographic Collection of Portraits of Nineteenth-Century Notables, 1862-1884.* Accessed on February 2, 2021. https://catalog.archives.gov/id/558770.

2. Battey, C. M. "W.E.B. (William Edward Burghardt) Du Bois." Accessed February 2, 2021. https://www.loc.gov/pictures/item/2003681451/.

3. Garrity, Mary. "Ida B. Wells." Accessed February 2, 2021. https://commons.wikimedia.org/wiki/File:Mary_Garrity_-_Ida_B._Wells-Barnett_-_Google_Art_Project_-_restoration_crop.jpg.

4. "Photograph of Harry Haywood." 1948. From Mark Solomon's *The Cry Was Unity: Communists and African Americans, 1917-1936.* Accessed on February 2, 2021. https://en.wikipedia.org/wiki/File:Harry_Haywood,_1948.jpg.

5. "Photograph of Hubert Harrison." Image Courtesy of the Schomburg Center for Research in Black Culture, The New York Public Library. Accessed on February 2, 2021. https://www.blackpast.org/african-american-history/harrison-hubert-henry-1883-1927/.

6. "Photograph of Cyril Briggs." Accessed on February 2, 2021. https://en.wikipedia.org/wiki/Cyril_Briggs#/media/File:Briggs-Cyril.jpg.

7. Payne, Daniel A. "Richard Allen." From the frontispiece of *History of the African Methodist Episcopal Church.* 1891. Accessed on February 2, 2021. https://en.wikipedia.org/wiki/Richard_Allen_(bishop)#/media/File:Richard_Allen_crop.jpg.

8. "Portrait of Sarah Bass Allen." Accessed on February 2, 2021. http://www.pbs.org/wgbh/aia/part3/3h476b.html.

9. "Photograph of Martin Robinson Delany." Accessed on February 2, 2021. https://en.wikipedia.org/wiki/Martin_Delany#/media/File:Martin_Robison_Delany_(before_1885).jpg.

10. "Grace Campbell addressing a Harlem Rally." Accessed on February 2, 2021. https://www.blackpast.org/african-american-history/campbell-grace-p-1883-1943/.

11. "Gastonia, N.C. Loray Cotton Mill (57,000 Spindles)." *Durwood Barbour Collection of North Carolina Postcards* (P077), North Carolina Collection Photographic Archives, Wilson Library, UNC-Chapel Hill. Accessed on February 2, 2021. https://dc.lib.unc.edu/cdm/ref/collection/nc_post/id/1272.

12. "Smith Act Defendants." From the personal collection of Frank Chapman.

Works Cited

(1900) W.E.B. Du Bois, "To the Nations of the World.'" *Black Past.* Accessed September 7, 2020. https://www.blackpast.org/african-american-history/1900-w-e-b-du-bois-nations-world/.

"Beal Blames Mill Forces For Recent Strike Outrage." *The Gastonia Daily Gazette.* April 20, 1929.

"Wilmington Red Shirts." *The Raleigh News and Observer.* November 4, 1898.

Abernathy, Ralph David, and Hosea Hudson. *Black Worker in the Deep South: A Personal Record.* International Publishers, 1972.

Akuno, Kali, and Ajamu Nangwaya, eds. *Jackson Rising: The Struggle for Economic Democracy and Black Self-determination in Jackson, Mississippi.* Daraja Press, 2017.

Allen, James S. *Reconstruction: The Battle for Democracy.* International Publishers, 1937.

Allen, James S., and Phillip Foner. eds. *American Communism and Black Americans: A Documentary History, 1919-1929.* Temple University Press, 1987.

Césaire, Aimé. *Discourse on Colonialism.* Monthly Review Press, 2001.

Cohen, Shari. "The Lasting Legacy of An American Dilemma." *Carnegie Results.* Carnegie Corporation of New York, 2004. Accessed December 11, 2020. https://www.carnegie.org/publications/lasting-legacy-american-dilemma/.

Cole, Peter. *Ben Fletcher: The Life and Times of a Black Wobbly.* Charles H. Kerr Publishing Company, 2007.

Degras, Jane, ed. *The Communist International, 1919-1943.* Vol. 1. Oxford University Press, 1956.

Delany, Martin Robison, et al. "Political Destiny of the Colored Race, on the American Continent." *Proceedings of the National Emigration Convention of Colored People, held at Cleveland, Ohio, August 24, 1854.* A. A. Anderson, 1854. Accessed October 22, 2020. https://omeka.coloredconventions.org/items/show/314.

Delany, Martin Robison. *The Condition, Elevation, Emigration, and Destiny of the Colored People of the United States and Official Report of the Niger Valley Exploring Party.* Humanity Books, 2008.

Dimitrov, Georgi. *The United Front: The Struggle Against Fascism and War.* Intentional Publishers, 1938.

Douglas, Frederick. *The Life and Times of Frederick Douglas.* Collier-MacMilllan, 1962.

Du Bois, W.E.B. *Black Reconstruction in America 1860-1880.* The Free Press, 1999.

Du Bois, W.E.B. *Color and Democracy: Colonies and Peace.* Harcourt Brace & Co., 1945.

Du Bois, W.E.B. *Souls of Black Folk.* Taylor & Francis, 2015.

Du Bois, W.E.B. *The Negro.* Cosimo, Inc., 2010.

Dutt, Palme. *Fascism and Social Revolution: A Study of the Economics and Politics of the Extreme Stages of Capitalism in Decay.* International Publishers, 1935.

Equal Justice Institute. "Lynching in America: Confronting the Legacy of Racial Terror." Accessed September 1, 2020. https://eji.org/reports/lynching-in-america/.

Foner, Eric. *Reconstruction: America's Unfinished Revolution, 1863-1877.* Harper, 2011.

Foner, Phillip. *Essays In Afro-American History.* Temple University Press, 1978.

Foner, Phillip. "The IWW and the Black Worker." *The Journal of Negro History.* 55. No. 1. 1970. Accessed September 28, 2020.

Foner, Phillip. *History of the Labor Movement in the United States Volume I: From Colonial Times to the Founding of the American Federation of Labor.* International Publishers, 1947.

Foner, Phillip. *Organized Labor and the Black Worker, 1619-1973.* International Publishers, 1976.

Foner, Phillip. *The Life and Writings of Frederick Douglass.* 4 vols. International Publishers, 1975.

Foster, William Z. *History of the Communist Party of the United States.* International Publishers, 1952

Foster, William Z. *The Negro People in American History.* International Publishers, 1976.

Gilmore, Glenda Elizabeth. *Defying Dixie: The Radical Roots of Civil Rights, 1919-1950.* W.W. Norton, 2009.

Graham, Nicholas. "June 1929: Strike at Loray Mill," *NC Miscellany.* June 1, 2004. https://blogs.lib.unc.edu/ncm/2004/06/01/this_month_june_1929/.

Haywood, Harry. *Black Bolshevik: Autobiography of an Afro-American Communist.* Liberator Press, 1978.

Haywood, Harry. *Negro Liberation.* Liberator Press, 1972.

Home, Gerald. *The Counter-Revolution of 1776: Slave Resistance and the Origins of the United States of America.* New York University Press, 2014.

House Committee on Un-American Activities. *The American Negro in the Communist Party.* U.S. Government Printing Office, 1954.

James, Winston. *Holding Aloft the Banner of Ethiopia*. Verso Books, 2020.

Kelley, Robin D. G. *Hammer and Hoe: Alabama Communists During the Great Depression*. University of North Carolina Press, 1990.

Lenin, V. I. *Collected Works*. 45 vols. Progress Publishers, 1977.

Lenin, V.I. *Selected Works*. Progress Publishers, 1963. 3 vols. Accessed August 30, 2020. https://www.marxists.org/archive/lenin/works/sw/index.htm.

Luxemburg, Rosa. *The Essential Rosa Luxemburg*. Haymarket Books, 2008.

Marable, Manning. *Race, Reform and Rebellion: The Second Reconstruction and Beyond in Black America, 1945-2006*. 3rd ed. University Press of Mississippi, 2007.

Marx, Karl, and Friedrich Engels. *A Contribution to the Critique of Political Economy*. Translated by S.W. Ryazanskaya. Progress Publishers, 1977. Accessed July 2, 2020. https://www.marxists.org/archive/marx/works/1859/critique-pol-economy/preface.htm.

Marx, Karl, and Friedrich Engels. *Karl Marx and Frederick Engels: Selected Works: In Three Volumes*. 3 vols. Progress Publishers, 1969. Accessed July 21, 2020. https://www.marxists.org/archive/marx/works/1848/communist-manifesto/ch01.htm.

Marx, Karl, and Friedrich Engels. *The Civil War in the United States*. Edited by Andrew Zimmerman. International Publishers, 2016.

Marx, Karl. *Theories of Surplus Value: Volume IV of Capital*. Progress Publishers, 197. Accessed July 23, 2020. https://www.marxists.org/archive/marx/works/1863/theories-surplus-value/.

Marx, Karl. *Capital: Volume I*. Translated by Samuel Moore and Edward Aveling. Edited by Frederick Engels. Progress Publishers. Accessed July 2, 2020. https://www.marxists.org/archive/marx/works/1867-c1/ch31.htm.

Marx, Karl. *Capital: Volume II.* Translated by Ernest Untermann. Edited by Friedrich Engels. Charles H. Kerr, 1907.

Marx, Karl. *The Civil War in France.* English edition of 1871. Accessed July 23, 2020. https://www.marxists.org/archive/marx/works/1871/civil-war-france/ch06.htm.

Marx, Karl. The Poverty of Philosophy. Translated by the Institute of Marxism Leninism. Progress Publishers, 1955. Accessed July 22, 2020, https://www.marxists.org/archive/marx/works/1847/poverty-philosophy/ch02.htm.

Messer-Kruse, Timothy. *Yankee International: Marxism and the American Reform Tradition.* University of North Carolina Press, 1998.

Reed, Adolf Jr. "Race and Class in the Work of Oliver Cromwell Cox," *Monthly Review.* 52. No. 9. 2001. Accessed December 11, 2020. https://monthlyreview.org/2001/02/01/race-and-class-in-the-work-of-oliver-cromwell-cox/.

Robinson, Cedric J. *Black Marxism: The Making of the Black Radical Tradition.* University of North Carolina Press, 2005.

Rosenman, Samuel I., ed. *Public Papers and Addresses of Franklin D. Roosevelt, vol. 2, The Year of Crisis, 1933.* Random House, 1938.

Second Congress of the Communist International: Minutes and Proceedings. Translated by Bob Archer. 2 vols. New Park Publications, 1977. https://www.marxists.org/history/international/comintern/2nd-congress.

Solomon, Mark. *The Cry Was Unity: Communists and African Americans, 1917-1936.* University Press of Mississippi, 1998.

Sorel, Jeff. "Black Reconstruction and the Paris Commune: Two Momentous Revolutions." *Workers World.* February 15, 2017. https://www.workers.org/2017/02/29723/.

Stalin, Joseph. *Collected Works.* Foreign Languages Publishing House, 1953.

Stalin, Joseph. *The Foundations of Leninism*. Foreign Languages Press, 1965.

Trotsky, Leon. *The First 5 Years of the Communist International*. Monad Press, 1972.

United States Code. Title 42. Chapter 21. Subchapter 1. Sections 1981–1985. Accessed on January 28, 2021. https://uscode.house.gov/browse/prelim@title42/chapter21/subchapter1&edition=prelim.

United States v. Cruikshank, 92 U.S. 542 (1875).

United States v. Price, 383 U.S. 787 (1966).

Washington, Booker T. *Up From Slavery: An Autobiography*. Doubleday, Page & Company, 1907.

Wells, Ida B. "Lynch Law in America", *The Arena*. 23. No. 1. January 1900. Accessed September 1, 2020. https://www.digitalhistory.uh.edu/disp_textbook.cfm?smtID=3&psid=1113.

Zinn, Howard. *A People's History of the United States: Abridged Teaching Edition*. New Press, 2003.